Using the Basic Skills Standards for ESOL

Acknowledgements

Much of the background work to this book in aggregating ideas, examples, and comments was carried out by Wee Kheng Marfell and Pauline Thomas, Basic Skills tutors at Gloucestershire College of Arts and Technology (Gloscat). They have been working on the ALBSU Special Development Project *'Developing ESOL in non-traditional settings'* with Liz Pill, the project co-ordinator, at Gloscat.

Gloscat was the site of the initial project in open flexible resource-based learning for ESOL and has supported its subsequent development. English Learning Centre (1989-1992).

Providers and practitioners nationally have been extremely co-operative in sharing ideas for this book.

Thanks are due to:

Hackney Community College, ESOL Service.

Ell Jaggi and Ann Jansen at 'Making Training Work'.

Pat Hyett – Allied Steel and Wire, Cardiff.

Philippa Williams – The Friary Centre, Cardiff.

Jill Manley – 3793/94 Verifier.

ESOL and Basic Skills Service at Gloscat.

The NATECLA Accreditation Working Party.

Sutton West Centre, ESOL Service.

English Language Service, Leicestershire County Council.

Training for Work, Peterborough College.

ESOL Service, The Davenport Centre, Stockport.

© The Adult Literacy and Basic Skills Unit,
7th Floor, Commonwealth House, 1-19 New Oxford Street, London WC1A 1NU.

ISBN 1 85990 003 8

Design: Studio 21

Published May 1994

Contents

1 | Introduction

What are the Standards anyway?

Most people know the ALBSU Standards through Wordpower which are widely used in education and in training situations to accredit adults and young people with competence in basic skills.

These basic skills such as:

- reading textual material

- reading graphical material

- completing forms

- writing notes, letters and expressive ideas

- conversing to provide and obtain information

are related to everyday activities for home and work.

The name 'Wordpower' has been given to this 3793 City and Guilds qualification and 'Numberpower' to the 3794 numeracy equivalent qualification.

The ALBSU Standards were developed as the result of the Basic Skills Accreditation Initiative (BSAI) funded jointly by the Department of Education and Science and the Employment Department. Under this initiative **Standards** for competence in basic skills were produced from work commissioned by ALBSU. These standards form the basis of the competence statements; the corresponding performance criteria; and the necessary underpinning knowledge and understanding, that such competence would require. Two examining boards, City and Guilds and the London Chamber of Commerce, offer accreditation through Wordpower and Numberpower Certificates.

In the accreditation students can prove their competence at different levels:

- Foundation, Stage 1, Stage 2 and Stage 3.

Thus at Foundation level and Stage 1 a student can be accredited with competence in a range of tasks that demand an appropriate use of communication skills at a Pre-GCSE level. Foundation Level would demand skills that are pre-level 1 GNVQ. Wordpower Stage 2 and 3 are using skills related broadly to GNVQ 2 and 3.

ALBSU Standards	National Curriculum	GNVQ Core Skills
Communication	English	Communication Skills
Foundation	Level 2-3	
Level 1	Level 4-5	Level 1
Level 2	Level 6	Level 2
Level 3	Level 8	Level 3
Numeracy	Mathematics	Numeracy Skills
Foundation	Level 3	
Level 1	Level 4-5	Level 1
Level 2	Level 6	Level 2

Why do we need a Basic Skills accreditation for ESOL students?

It needs to be borne in mind that the competence statements relate to skills and not to the use of language itself. However, as they are **communication** skills the level of use of language will affect the ability to perform tasks competently.

Wordpower accreditation enables ESOL students to prove their skills performance on a par with mother tongue English speaking students. Employers, trainers and educators will then recognise the real value of the competence and ESOL students will not be continually marginalised by having to prove accurate language use even when performance does not require it.

A student can only prove language competence while performing a task which requires the use of language. To use the term 'using language competently' only has meaning if we follow it by 'in everyday life while performing everyday tasks'.

ESOL students should be given an opportunity to prove their abilities equally alongside mother tongue English speakers.

Why competence-based accreditation?

Most vocational qualifications are now expressed in terms of 'competence' statements – National Vocational Qualifications (NVQ). This allows students to practically demonstrate their ability to carry out a task which is one that would naturally need to be carried out in the vocational situation. A checklist of performance criteria enables the assessor to check that the task has been completed competently. These criteria define the minimum acceptable level of performance and each one must be demonstrated.

Evidence of the demonstration will also be needed.

Competence-based accreditation allows students to demonstrate learning and progress in a practical and natural way. Wordpower and Numberpower thus correspond well to such thinking and are recognised by the Further Education Funding Council (FEFC).

Wordpower provides a means to accredit students with their ability to carry out everyday tasks such as writing letters, making telephone calls, and following instruction manuals.

Wherever a task is performed it makes sense to look at whether the task is competently carried out. Did the letter carry the relevant information and could it be understood by the reader? Did the telephone call achieve its aim? Was the student able to act successfully on the instructions? If we **only** look at the structure of language used and its correctness we are overlooking the task in its entirety and what it aims to achieve. Thus in an arena of present day competence-based accreditation for vocational tasks it is sensible to do the same for everyday tasks. In fact such proof of competence is particularly relevant to speakers of other languages where it pays due attention to the successful completion of the task in hand.

However, this is an approach which will need sensitive handling by the tutor/ assessor. The student who is keen on the importance of an accurate use of language, and is striving for this, will rightly want feedback and correction. Where it is then understood that such a high level of accuracy was not in fact required for competence to be shown, the student will probably be satisfied, and can do any additional individual learning that he/she may be motivated to do.

What is competence?

Competence can be defined as *having sufficient skill and knowledge for a purpose*. In the case of Wordpower 'the purpose' is in the performance of everyday tasks. The skills and knowledge only have to be 'sufficient' for the purpose of carrying out the task.

Are the ALBSU Standards relevant to ESOL students?

The long term improver

It is likely that the student who comes for general improvement on a longer term basis will do many tasks in their learning programme which could be incidentally accredited. They may be concentrating on language development which itself would not be accredited but the tasks performed in the learning programme could be.

Naturally the appropriate level needs to be chosen but such students will inevitably, in practising using English, be writing letters, writing about events and personal experiences, and extracting information from texts and recorded voices all of which appear in the ALBSU Standards framework.

The Trainee

As part of the training programme the trainee will gain the underpinning knowledge and understanding for the vocational area, learn skills, and will need relevant and appropriate language in order to carry these out. Whether the trainee is studying on the training course, or learning and practising skills, many of these will be Wordpower and Numberpower accreditable. In some training programmes there is a special Wordpower slot created when all trainees on that course concentrate on doing tasks from worksheets which will lead to accreditation. This seems unnecessary if such competences are being proved within the context of the course itself.

The study support student

The ALBSU Standards framework and accreditation can be of value in the learning support situation where mainstream students are having additional support possibly in an open learning setting. As with the long term improver these students will be doing practice work and exercises that can be accredited incidentally. Often their mainstream coursework will also provide evidence of competence in certain skills areas. Under GNVQ the core skills will be accredited as part of their qualification. Using Wordpower would facilitate a separate accreditation for such skills also allowing them to be accredited at a lower level than GNVQ Level 1.

These different types of student need and the way in which accreditation could be used point to the importance of the **learning** being related to what the student really wants and needs while **accreditation** occurs more incidentally. However, it is also a good idea to provide accreditation as an incentive to learners who may be motivated by achieving and proving something. As long as the process demands learning along the way and does not just become an exercise in producing evidence of current competence then it can be a good motivational tool.

What Wordpower ISN'T

Wordpower provides a framework for Basic Skills. In this framework the communication skills are broken down into their components, are shown to interconnect, and are seen to accumulate and progress. Thus, for tutors, it has provides something tangible in which, and from which, to work. Skills that may have previously been learned and practised in isolation or overlooked now make sense as a whole. It becomes too easy then for us as tutors to rely on it as a syllabus, because we see that it gives structure to the learning where none may have previously existed. However, Wordpower and Numberpower are not syllabuses and should not be used as such in a learning programme. They are accreditation frameworks.

This does not mean that Wordpower cannot provide a valuable aid to tutors in assessing where a student may be already in the performance of basic skills.

As a framework which is visualised it can help in:

- 'placing' a student by current performance and giving a starting point to the learning programme

- pinpointing gaps in the student's skills

- giving pointers on what could be attainment goals

- providing a pathway of monitoring progress

- diagnosing why a student is not achieving 'competence'.

Such frameworks are meaningful to the tutor in pointing the way but not necessarily to the students who themselves will have individual needs and goals which will motivate their learning.

A learning programme for the student must therefore address individual needs and the step by step progression necessary for longer learning goals to be achieved. The Wordpower and Numberpower frameworks will assist in the start point, planning the learning and in monitoring the progress but cannot supply the syllabus.

The Standards provide a framework NOT a syllabus or learning programme.

What Wordpower IS

Wordpower and Numberpower are accreditation frameworks. Learning needs must be addressed separately in a learning programme. Accreditation can then happen incidentally as the student proves competence in the skills while following the learning programme.

Wordpower and Numberpower are well-known in educational, training and employment situations. This recognition is very important to students who will need such currency.

Because competence is built up over a period of time, working towards Wordpower certification can give an incentive to the student to keep learning. However, if it takes too long, students can become demotivated.

Because Wordpower allows accreditation at different levels of sophistication in terms of input from texts (spoken and written) and student output in the presentation of the spoken and written word, it can be flexibly used to accredit competence individually. Students studying together within the same short course group can be accredited at different levels.

Because students can gain accreditation for individual Units in Records of Achievement, rather than doing the whole certificate at a particular level, it is flexible enough to cope with individual needs and goals. Because it is competence-based it is acceptable in vocational work and will relate well to core skills competences in GNVQs.

Wordpower and Numberpower are nationally accepted accreditation schemes. They have currency for the students as they are recognised by, and meaningful to, educational, training and employment situations.

2 | Using the Standards in ESOL Programmes

The Basic Skills Accreditation Initiative identified at the common basic communication skills that were needed for everyday life at various levels of sophistication. It then analysed the ways in which competence for these could be accredited. There is no special mention made of speakers of other languages as the competence standards for all are uniform. Wordpower, therefore, must be made to work for ESOL students if they are going to compete on an equal footing in education, training and employment. There are ways in which we, as practitioners can hold on to the principles of learning which we have developed in our ESOL work but still open up this opportunity for accreditation to the students.

Addressing the Issues

These are some of the issues practitioners have raised:

> *1. Practitioners feel that many ESOL students already have and can easily prove competence in communication skills in mother tongue. Thus, such students find it boring and irrelevant to have to prove them at an inappropriate level because their current level of English restricts their proof of competence.*

In performing everyday tasks competently students are showing that they are using the English language, both spoken and written, in an appropriate and relevant way. The ability to carry out a communication task competently requires an underpinning knowledge of language in terms of words, expressions, and grammar at an appropriate level. It also requires the skills of assimilating, sifting and processing information from the written or spoken word (Input skills) and the skills of putting together information and presenting it in the written or spoken form so that it can be understood by the receiver. The level of language acquisition the student currently has will restrict the level of sophistication at which these skills can be proved. However, as all learning needs to be in context, ESOL students will continually be performing everyday tasks as a vehicle for acquiring and practising language. They will be proving their skills competence and it would be a shame if this was not being accredited in some way. If they are being accredited more incidentally, rather than centrally as an accreditation or learning programme, then the level of sophistication becomes less dominant as the student is more conscious of the language learning. This means that a tutor's worry that the student is well used to using skills at this level in mother tongue and it might therefore seem patronising for them to try out the task at this level becomes less important as the student sees the value of the use of language and is proving the skills competence incidentally. This also means that the practitioners' worry that students are proving competence at a stage that they have already reached, rather than that which they might attain, also becomes less important as these are proved incidentally while the student concentrates on language use and acquisition. This puts an onus on the tutor to select appropriate material and tasks for the student.

---

2. Do the ALBSU Standards place enough emphasis on listening and speaking?

At Foundation Level the spoken competence in Conversing with one other person (Unit 5) has 3 Elements to it:

- *5.1 Provide information to one person*

- *5.2 Obtain information from one person*

- *5.3 Hold a conversation with one person.*

*However, there are two units related to reading and **two** to writing.*

In any learning programme for ESOL students there is bound to be learning and practice in spoken skills. At a beginning level in particular these may demand much more time and effort than the oral competences would reflect. We may need to set other targets for students who are speakers of other langauges which reflect this time and effort.

Listening as a skill is also important and not separately accredited. This does not in itself undermine the accreditation as it exists which accredits two-way communication but does mean that we may need to provide additional assessments in our learning programme to satisfy both tutor and student that progress in **listening** is occuring. Listening and the accompanying skills are often overlooked in basic skills work generally.

This again highlights the need for us to be clear in the difference between the learning programme for the student that will address individual needs and goals and the accreditation or charting process related to basic communication skills. Listening must be a part of a learning programme. Wordpower does not provide a learning programme.

> *3. Are the competence steps small enough to be able to accredit language development?*

ESOL practitioners on the whole would much rather be able to recognise progress with ESOL students in much smaller steps. The underpinning knowledge and skills required for Unit 5, 'Conversing with one other person', reflect how much language learning would need to take place before the student could prove competence: being able to formulate questions verbally, to use tense appropriately and to show word order conventions. However, we have to remember that though this accreditation scheme is not language based, it does not stop us from being able to make a checklist of language usage that we would hope the student would demonstrate. This will satisfy our need to recognise smaller steps, help the student to see the relevance of the language acquisition and still enable the student to compete on an equal footing with mother-tongue English speakers.

> *4. As it may take time for an ESOL student to cover the underpinning language for competence to be shown, the whole accreditation process can be drawn out and demotivate the student.*

If we put more of an emphasis on incidental accreditation rather than the whole learning process being geared to reaching an accreditation goal then we would overcome this difficulty. There are some additional points:

- the onus is on the tutor to enter the student at an appropriate level so that it does not take disproportionately long to achieve.

- the checklist of language acquisition can be shared with the student to enable him/her to appreciate the progress that is being made in learning English.

- it is always possible to accredit individual units so that achievement is acknowledged without the student needing to strive without reward.

> *5. Practitioners feel that the Performance Criteria are difficult for speakers of other languages to understand.*

There is a great deal of variation in thought and practice in the field about the degree to which tutors feel that performance criteria should be shared and completely understood by students. Some programmes have carefully translated these criteria, and some have simplified them. Translation on its own does not necessarily improve the understanding as they may still need to be 'explained'. Other programmes feel that students should be allowed to demonstrate competence and subsequently share with them what particular skills and competence they have demonstrated. In these cases practitioners are clear about needing to make the task itself very explicit and in simple terms.

It seems important here to be sensitive to the student and client group. Sometimes students will respond to interpreting and analysing the performance criteria. Otherwise it may make the process unnecessarily cumbersome.

Where a mother tongue is shared by several students and there is a bilingual tutor on hand translation may be worthwhile. It is however very time intensive and costly. We have to be sure that there are realistic advantages in doing this and not just feel that translation is 'the answer'. It may not be. We may need rather to explore ways of explaining in simple English.

Tutors need to weigh up each individual case as to how appropriate a complete sharing of understanding the performance criteria is to the situation. The type of task, the student's current understanding of 'competence' and 'performance', and the value of the sharing for the individual student are all factors in this decision.

---

6. Have some programmes entered ESOL students at a lower level than is really appropriate to them because of their current level of use of English and because of funding availability which favours Foundation level?

Unfortunately, there are instances where students have been entered at an inappropriately low level because of funding availability which favours Foundation level. Students can become bored and disconnected from the relevance and justly lack motivation. Such use of Wordpower is not addressing students individual learning needs. If it were they would be motivated in their langauge aquisition and would be encouraged to perfect performance. The problem is not so much the level at which they are entered but more the quality of the learning opportunities that they are being offered. In a training situation it should be possible for trainees working together to be performing quite comfortably at different levels. The tasks do not need to be offered in separate 'Wordpower' sessions but can be integrated into the training programme.

Summary

- A learning programme for ESOL students must address spoken language needs. These may not appear as competences in Wordpower satisfying the tutor and student's need to demonstrate language development. This may mean having an additional checklist which enables us to tick off language items as they are demonstrated by the student.

14

- We need to distinguish between the learning programme which will address the underpinning knowledge and understanding needed and the demonstration of competence in carrying out an everyday communication task.

- The more incidental we can make the accreditation process to the students own learning programme the more meaningful, productive and satisfying the process will be.

- The degree to which there needs to be a sharing and understanding of performance criteria must be assessed for individual situations.

Assessing a competent performance

Performance Criteria

If we look at the performance criteria for Communication in Writing:

At Foundation Level

Grammar, spelling and punctuation have to be checked and corrected, as appropriate, **sufficiently for writing to be understood by the intended reader.**

At Stage 1

Grammar, spelling and punctuation are checked and corrected, as appropriate, **sufficiently to maintain the confidence of the intended reader.**

At Stage 2

Spelling, grammar, and punctuation **appropriate for audience and purpose are used.**

These imply that at Foundation Level the level of accuracy is superceded by the importance of the message being understood. As long as inaccuracies in grammar, spelling and punctuation do not interfere with the understanding of the gist of the writing then competence has been achieved. Language inaccuracies could be quite high and still not impede understanding of the meaning.

At Stage 1 there is a demand for an accuracy level which would hold the attention of the intended reader. This implies that the reader is not required to read and reread several times in order to sort out word order and meaning. The meaning is understood without effort on the part of the reader.

The student also has to demonstrate a level of sophistication which shows 'purpose' by making a choice over appropriate language. Any minor inaccuracies in the use of vocabulary, word order and grammar will be insignificant amongst the appropriate use of language for the purpose.

Fluency and Accuracy

It is important for ESOL students to appreciate the distinction between fluency and accuracy. In some communication tasks such as 'Holding a Conversation with one person' (Foundation Level) fluency in putting over ideas will be important. Where personal information is being given or particular instructions, on the other hand there will be a need for accuracy. In this second case the student's acknowledgement of and demonstration of the place of accuracy will be important. For instance, in giving personal information it may be necessary to use a past tense to convey the meaning. A student's choice of words or attempts at self-correction will demonstrate an appreciation of the need for accuracy.

When we are assessing a student's performance we need to weigh up first the relative importance of accuracy and fluency in that particular situation and if appropriate share it with the student.

- The type of task will dictate the level of accuracy required. We may expect a higher level of accuracy in a letter or written message which had to communicate something specific than in a free writing passage which was showing an expression of ideas and feelings.

- The arena for performance or the situation in which the task is being performed will also dictate the level of accuracy required. Different standards of performance may be tolerated in a family corner shop from those expected in a high street store.

The task

It is important to assess the task as a whole and to focus on this. Was the task completed successfully? Because the only guidance we are given in the performance criteria relates to the intended audience we have to decide on the arena for performance and what sort of performance we would anticipate as competent in that arena. A handwritten message left for someone on the shop floor would need to convey the message adequately but considerable tolerance in use of language could be exercised. However, in the business office environment such tolerance may not be possible. So notes to colleagues (Element 4.1) is influenced by the arena for performance. Sometimes it is too easy, particularly in the training situation where office work predominates, to set unfair standards for performance even at Foundation level because of the anticipated arena. By concentrating on the task itself, and what it aims to do, and by using the range statements and performance criteria as guidance we can avoid this. It seems to be a mistake to 'start' by getting bogged down in the criteria. They become most useful when trying to analyse **why** a performance is **not** competent.

How do you assess?

It is important not to put an additional barrier in the way for proof of competence. If we are asking students to *write* answers to questions about the content of a text in order to assess understanding, we are then inadvertently assessing their writing *(production)* skills and not their reading *(receptive)* skills. Sometimes it may be most appropriate to do it this way but we must be conscious of the ways in which assessment could be clouded because of this.

Asking questions verbally about the content and understanding of a text may give a truer assessment, providing we use simplified language if necessary. Verbal questioning allows one to be flexible and responsive to the student and the moment.

It is a good idea to ask students to point to or highlight the relevant bit of text which they are referring to when answering the questions. This not only provides the assessor with tangible evidence of the way in which the student is doing the task but is also very good study skills training for the student.

Using Mother Tongue

It is possible to use mother tongue in assessment provided the programme has mother tongue speakers available. This would, of course, be the most appropriate and fair way of assessing certain competences particularly at Foundation Level. For the Reading Units, Unit 1: Reading textual material and Unit 2: Reading Graphical Material for Everyday purposes, it would make sense to ask verbal questions in mother tongue to gauge whether or not the student has understood and can act or report on the main points. Otherwise we will be testing the students competence in presenting answers in English and not their competence in reading. However, such bilingual support is not widely enough available so we need to examine ways in which we can make the assessments as 'fair' as possible for the speaker of another language. We need to be aware of the way in which their use of language might be interfering with our assessment of competence. We need to be sure of what we are assessing.

Example of Reading Assessment

The example shown on page 18 with tutor's comments shows:

- How the students' knowledge of the context and vocabulary has affected assessment
- how useful mother tongue was in the assessment process.

Who can assess?

- Maybe we rely too much on using the teachers and trainers involved in the learning situation to assess students' performance. Let us consider other possibilities.

Using fellow students

In some of the Units interaction between students can be used to facilitate demonstration of competence and also enable the students, who are not yet ready

Reading textual material

R1B
FOUNDATION LEVEL

Element 1: **Extracting the main idea from a piece of text**

A reading assessment done as part of a review of the learning progress of a Chinese speaking student at the beginner level - This shows the effect the context and students general knowledge will have on an assessment

---

WEST ROAD INFANTS SCHOOL

is holding its

SPRING JUMBLE SALE

on Saturday 10th April

Starting at 2.00pm
Entry is free

Please bring any jumble to the school on Saturday morning. If you have any big items we will be happy to collect.

Just ring Ann on 62374.

→ doesn't know the meaning of the word

→ needs explaining

Does'nt know meaning of word but guesses from context

understands this and can explain to tutor in M.T.

unaware it's a name ←

Knows its a telephone number

Tutor's Comment

Student read this and was able to answer some questions about it in her M.T. She knew this was a notice of some event held by the West Road Infant school. but couldn't say precisely what the event was. She was able to state the time and day of the event as well as explain the paragraph regarding contributions. She would, however, have failed this assessment if she was not able to express her understanding the text in her mother-tongue and had to answer questions in English instead.

themselves to demonstrate competence, to become familiar with performance criteria. Unless students are given the opportunity to watch for and interpret body language for instance they will not see the relevance of it in their own performance. Thus someone who is still in the learning and practising phase for a particular competence could be given the opportunity to assess another student.

Example:

Elements 10.1 and 10.2

10.2 Obtaining information from one person

A student needs to go to the nearby minibus hire firm and find out about a journey to Durham for a family event. An accompanying student as witness is asked to:

1. note how the student started with the enquiry (10.2.1.)

2. see whether the information needed is obtained (10.2.2.)

3. notice any difficulties in understanding and how they were overcome (10.2.3/5/6)

4. watch for facial expressions and gestures (10.2.5.)

Reporting back on this to the tutor as a witness provides evidence and a learning process for the witness.

10.1 Providing information to one person

This same student witness can then also receive this repeated information from the enquiring student with the reasons for the journey being made and the way in which the journey will be carried out. (10.2.8. and all 10.1).

Using other witnesses

These could be colleagues in the workplace or family members. Where such evidence is being used it is beneficial to provide a checklist to the witness.

Using the student's own reported evidence

In view of the fact that Wordpower has been designed to accredit everyday activities we must in some way enable the collection of student actual and reported evidence on

Can you make a phone call?

- **Ring the cinema (see previous sheet). Find out:**

1. What film is on tonight?
   (If more than one choose one)

   ....

2. What time the film starts?

   ....

3. How much it costs to get in?

   ....

4. How many days is it on for?

   ....

WP1 U5 E2 – *Aims*

- find out if the person who answers can help you
- if they cannot, get the correct person or arrange to ring back
- ask questions in a sensible order
- use suitable language
- use a suitable tone of voice
- if you do not understand, ask them to repeat
- get the information you want

what they do away from the teaching situation. In this instance we very much need to concentrate on evidence of successful completion of a task and whether it achieved what it set out to do. We cannot always expect to be able to check whether all performance criteria have been met for every and each demonstration of competence. Once students are familiar with the Standards and the accreditation they themselves might spot when they are proving competence. As tutors become more familiar with using it they find inobtrusive ways of finding out if performance criteria are satisfied.

Right from the beginning in any basic skills work students should be encouraged to share their out-of-class life and the relevance this has to learning. This helps to pass the onus for learning, and in the case of Wordpower the collection of evidence and relevant practice materials, on to the student.

WORKPLACE ASSESSMENT FOR WORDPOWER

Student/Trainee's Name: ...... *ALFRED JONES* ....

College Group: ...... *Tuesday Evening* ....

Workplace Assessor's Name: ...... *Mr Roy Francis* ....

Thank you for agreeing to witness ...... *Alfred* ...... doing certain tasks at work will provide evidence for accrediting City and Guilds Wordpower to this student/trainee.

The student/trainee has identified the tasks he/she does at work which relate to the certificate and they are listed on these sheets. You are asked to watch to see that he/she carries out these tasks competently using reading, writing, speaking and listening skills. We have provided you with a checklist which helps you to look for the way in which the task is carried out. Please will you tick each item to show us that you have seen the student/trainee do it in that way. Do not tick unless you are satisfied that you have seen or heard it. Please sign each sheet separately.

Thank you for your help.

Alice Smith
Tutor

In all these cases we may feel it important to double check assessments out of concern that the witnesses are not competent assessors. However, as long as one instance of the competence has been carefully evidenced it seems important that a flexibility of approach be encouraged in the other instances. This will cut down on the tutor involvement time, prevent us from relying too much on simulated tasks and will encourage students to take more responsibility themselves in the process. It is important to concentrate on successful completion of task. When we think in this way it becomes easier to accept other people as being 'competent' assessors of this success.

ELEMENT OF COMPETENCE

Reading Signs and Labels – (Unit 2 Element 1)

Student's identified workplace task:

> Labels on disinfectant
>
> Safety signs for tractor

Checklist

I have noted that the student/trainee

- looked at the signs/labels to understand them ☐

- thought about them to make sense of them ☐

- reported back correctly to me about what they meant ☐

- acted correctly on the information given by the sign/label ☐

Signed by assessor in workplace:

....

ELEMENT OF COMPETENCE

Extract Information from Tables – (Unit 2 Element 3)

Student/Trainee's
identified workplace task:

"Worming" of poultry
dogs

Choosing doseages
from tables

Checklist

I have noted that the student/trainee

- knew what sort of information was required from the tables ☐

- looked through the table carefully to search information ☐

- found the relevant information ☐

- knew how to then use and act on this information ☐

Signed by assessor in workplace:

....

ELEMENT OF COMPETENCE

Follow pictorial instructions to carry out an activity – (Unit 2 Element 4)

Student's identified workplace task:

> Cleaning dairy equipment
> Using instructions for
> cleaning fluid from
> pictures

Checklist

I noted that the student/trainee

- selected all the necessary equipment ☐

- used the pictures to help decide which order to do the task ☐

- used the pictures to clarify how to do it ☐

- completed the task successfully ☐

Signed by assessor in workplace:

....

Using the workplace

Demonstration of competence in the workplace is extermely important as it gives everyday occupational relevance to the competence. If the workplace supervisor is provided with easy and comprehensive instructions and a checklist it is not onerous and time consuming. However, student, employer, and supervisor have to be agreeable to this.

How does Wordpower relate to other accreditation schemes?

Other accreditation schemes which are currently being used in ESOL programmes are the RSA Profile Certificate and Pitman ESOL. There are also programmes where competence-based Open College accreditation is being used.

RELATING THE ALBSU STANDARDS TO PITMAN'S ESOL

READING TASKS

Pitman Paper	Task	Standards equivalent
103, 106, 107	Reading instructions for listening part	6.2
104	Read and extract information – put on to form	6.1
106, 107	Read and act on signs by finding appropriate text	7.1
	Read through form to establish what is required	3.1. 8.1

WRITING TASKS

Pitman Paper	Task	Standards equivalent
107, 104	Writing a message	4.1
106	Fill in a form	3.2
105, 102	Write about yourself, your family, etc	4.2

Generally the reading tasks require skills at Stage 1 of the ALBSU Standards whereas the writing tasks are at Foundation level. Form filling exercise could be at Foundation or Stage 1.

Oral communication in the listening part of the Pitman ESOL exam relates more to the skills expected at Stage 1. However, in the **Speaking exam**, taken separately, and which is also at 5 levels, Level 1 (Basic) and Foundation level of the Standards match well.

SPEAKING EXAM

Basic	Give personal information, obtain information hold a conversation	5.1, 5.2, 5.3

ESOL – 106 (PITMAN)

READING – Part 3

Read the facts about a famous footballer and then fill in the table using the information.

Bobby Scott, the captain of Trensham Football Team was born in Dulwich on 5 May 1972. His father, John Scott, is a doctor and his mother, Linda, is a teacher. He has two sisters who are both at college. They try to watch their brother play when they can. His first club was Harlow United but now he is at Trensham where he plays centre-forward. As well as football he likes to play tennis and go sailing. He has his own small boat which he loves. He isn't married yet.

FOOTBALL FACT FILE

First Name: .... Surname: ....

First Football Club: ....

Present Club: ....

Date of Birth: .... Age: ....

Place of Birth: ....

Father's Name and Job: ....

Mother's Name and Job: ....

Number in Family: ....

Hobbies: ....

Married/Single: ....

Basic (Level 1) Pitman ESOL that requires reading skills and information sorting at near Stage 1 of the Standards, but form filling at Foundation Level. (3.1, 3.2).

As Wordpower is nationally known and has greater currency in the employment market, it makes sense to be looking for ways in which the evidence collected for the other accreditation could be cross referenced to Wordpower should the student need it. Obviously where these are competence-based it is relatively easy.

Pitman ESOL, which is exam-based but can be taken flexibly at any time, is examined at 5 levels. At the Basic Level 1 the tasks given to students can also prove competence for Foundation or Stage 1 Wordpower.

In any learning situation the incidental accumulation of evidence will enable the student to build up a portfolio which could at any time be built upon to gain the Wordpower certificate. Such evidence may also be of use to the student if he/she progresses on to a mainstream course.

The core skills for GNVQ relate well to certain Wordpower competences (see chart on page 6). An interaction between these could give a student an additional pathway to gaining accreditation.

3 | Where's the learning in all this?

With all the emphasis on the students proving that they can use basic communication skills to competently perform tasks in everyday life there is a danger that we might be just trying to accredit students with what they can do now and not build in any expectation of learning. Any speaker of another language will be keen to improve their mastery of the English language and we have to bear this constantly in mind. Each ESOL student has a right to feel that his/her personal language development will be catered for.

It may not be enough to think that because students are using language in their study or training that they will inevitably pick up and improve on their use of language in this process. Thus, we might think that if they are 'doing Wordpower' they must be learning some new and useful language along the way. However, we cannot assume that the acquisition of language is random. The student is relying on us, as 'experts', to pick out for them the ways in which their current experience and use of language is holding them back or hindering them in their expression of themselves and demonstration of their skills. They also have a right to feel that we, as 'experts', are going to help them improve and develop their use of English so that they can reach their full potential.

We have already established that Wordpower as an accreditation scheme, should be used as incidentally as possible to the learning situation. Each student will come with their own learning goals which will demand a mixture of language development and the improvement of skills and knowledge. If they are on a training course or vocational course there will also be learning demands for this. The students have to rely on us to guide them in their learning. We need to spot and help them to recognise where the learning of language, the practice of a skill or the assimilation of information will help them to achieve the goals. Hence the initial assessment of exactly what a student can and can't do at the beginning of their time with us is crucial to the whole process.

Initial Assessment

This needs to give the tutor information about:

- the student's current use of English
- the likely level of basic skills development which the student has in mother tongue

- the probable level of study skills already acquired by the student

- the likely level of skills possessed as related to either the vocational area and/or the learning goals of the student

- the general knowledge that the student already has about the vocational area and/or about life and the systems in Britain.

There is a difference in approach here for speakers of other languages. This is because the students' current use of language may cloud our judgement in initial assessment of their abilities. We need to try and sort out the difficulties that may exist for the student because of a lack of language, as opposed to the difficulties that may exist in their ability to input and process information in a spoken or written form. The students who have never acquired information processing skills in mother tongue, either because they are not literate in mother tongue, or because they have had little or no schooling, cannot be expected to have those in English.

The easiest way to sort out English language development level as opposed to skills development would be to assess skills in mother tongue. Sometimes in the training situation this is essential as, if the assessment of vocational skills is made in English, the students own understanding and use of English could give an entirely false picture. If we do not have this assessment facility with bilingual staff, and most of us do not, we have to try and build up a picture by taking clues from the information we receive: clues from their schooling, clues from their previous work experience, clues from the way they appear to handle information and clues from the way in which they present information.

We have to decide how best we can help the student to reach learning goals. Part of any learning programme for speakers of other languages should include the development of language from where they are at present.

The student's current understanding and use of language

Most language text books will follow a fairly standard plan for teaching language:

- vocabulary
- grammar structures
  word order to convey meaning
  - Subject – verb – object
  - position of adverbs etc.
  - positive/negative statements

  use of particular structures to convey meaning
  - use of auxiliary verbs
  - 'do' in negatives and questions

- modals
- passives
- conditionals

changes in verbs to make tenses
- continuous and simple tenses
- using 'have' in past

- expressions or language functions as specific groups of words together that have particular meaning and which we would not necessarily just deduce from our knowledge of vocabulary and grammar. These have to be learnt and applied.

e.g. functions for apologising
- I'm sorry . . .
- Please forgive me . . .
- I'm afraid that . . .

making an invitation
- Would you like to come to . . .
- I would like you to . . .
- Please can you . . .

Such a framework is useful at initial assessment to 'place' the student in terms of the English language and language awareness already acquired. If the student is showing some use of tense but it is often incorrect or inappropriate and affecting the communication adversely then some learning around tense would be sensible.

For the student who shows no understanding of the importance of word order and is not using 'don't' in a negative but is saying 'I no like' then he/she really needs to learn and practise this before any further progress can be made.

The student who seems to speak and write fairly competently but is not yet using the passive should spend time in learning and practising this as the next step. He/she may get by very well on the training course or in completing the Wordpower certificate without it, but this would not be helping the personal language development.

Planning the learning

Mostly we tend to group reading and writing skills together and then listening and speaking. However, it is important to recognise the relationship between reading and listening as being **input** or **receptive** skills and writing and speaking as being **output** or **productive** skills.

the quality and range of resources available to tutors and trainers, and easy access to them, is extremely important.

The resources should

- cover a range of needs
  - grammar
  - topics
  - basic skills
  - study skills
- cover a range of levels (some of the advanced EFL books can provide valuable listening material which can also be used for mother tongue English speakers)
- be as familiar as possible to the tutors
- be arranged and organised in a way which makes them easy to access for both tutors and students.

It is really important that the student knows what he/she is actually trying to achieve at any one moment in the learning programme.

Students need to be clear about

1. when they are acquiring knowledge and understanding from the resources (i.e. they are learning **how to do something** and therefore expect to extract what they need from them) – an INPUT of knowledge.

2. when they are **practising** something to make themselves familiar and comfortable in using the knowledge for 1).

3. when they are being assessed as being competent at doing it.

Thus, in the learning programme it would be helpful if this is clear for the student. It is also important that the student learns the value of reference sources and as soon as possible learns to use and rely on these.

Dictionaries are vital and every ESOL student should be encouraged to buy his/her own and have it available. These should also be available in the teaching situation but an individually owned copy is really essential to the student's learning.

Reference Grammar books are also essential and should be available at all levels.

Other reference books will provide standard letter language, essay language, functional language (of apology, complaint etc.). Students should be encouraged not to feel guilty about relying on these. There is nothing wrong in searching out a standard expression and using it. We are doing it all the time – borrowing language from television, radio, newspapers and friends. Such use of reference material is very good training for the students.

PLANNING THE LEARNING

Element 16.1 (Stage 2)

Explain or describe orally an activity, place or object to help one person or several people to do something.

TASK for student W. which will be used to assess this competence

To describe to a group of students how they should perform a simple experiment with beetroot or red cabbage. The experiment requires that they add vinegar and bicarbonate of soda to pieces of beetroot and note what happens. This task demands that W. use visual aids to demonstrate but should use language of instruction clearly with pronunciation and stress as appropriate to make instructions clear. The students in the group can then demonstrate that they are obtaining information from a live talk or lecture (Element 12.1) and reporting on what happened in written or spoken form (9.2 and 10.1)

Programme of learning for student W.

1. **Underpinning language needed**

   Explanation/description sequential – First . . . then . . .

   Instruction Take . . . then . . . Put . . .

   Ref . . . Book name to be added

2. **Vocabulary**

   Of equipment and prepositions – student to reference dictionary and check with volunteer.

3. **Practice for student W.**

   Record on tape recorder, listen back and note pronunciation, stress on instruction words.

   Practise a couple of times. Ask someone to listen through the recording with you and comment.

   Assessment Date: 16.4.93

   Time: 1.00pm

   Other Students: May, Su Li, Rashida, Violet

Making up the certificate

Although there needs to be an emphasis on individual learning needs and fitting accreditation around them, it is also a good idea to allow and facilitate opportunities for students to make up the elements/units that thay may have overlooked in this programme. In this way they can gain the whole certificate. This demands that some worksheet/task resources available to tutors and students are also arranged and organised with this in mind. If a section of the resources are marked individually with which units/elements are covered when these pieces of work are completed, the students themselves can choose a task that appeals to them.

4 | Using the Basic Skills Standards with ESOL students

We can profitably examine the way in which the Standards can be used for ESOL students by grouping the students according to their reasons for coming to the ESOL provision i.e. their longer term learning goals. The students are categorised:

- the **long term improvers**. They may not come for an especially long period of time but they are on a continuum of progression and learning

- the **trainees** who are on a training course but want and need language

- the students who come for a **specific purpose** and a shorter term learning goal

- the students who are having language support for mainstream courses in a **learning/study** support system.

THE STANDARDS AND THE LONG TERM IMPROVER

For ESOL students who are long term improvers their main motivation will come from a desire to generally improve their use of English for whatever they are doing or want to do in life.

Thus, we would expect the learning outcomes to show improvement:

- in the grammatical and structural use of English

- in applying that language to particular situations

- in using that language in the performance of tasks.

It is at this point that we can see the relevance of a competence-based measure of performance for speakers of other languages. They will be acquiring language but will want to practise and assess that use of language in context, i.e. in a situation or in performing a task. Therefore, each time they come to practise their language learning and acquisition they will do it in a way in which their basic communication skills competence can be assessed. It is therefore relevant and important that they are given the chance to gain accreditation by this means – incidentally within their learning programme.

Goal setting

As the intention would be to allow more incidental accreditation, goal setting and the identification of short term learning goals becomes very important.

We need to be certain of identifying learning needs. These will be:

- language needs as related to
  - any gaps in current use of English
  - any personal goal needs
  - the expected development of language for the individual

- basic skills needs

- study skills needs

- knowledge needs as related to the task in hand or understanding the way life functions in Britain.

Some of these short term learning goals are likely to be communication skill and task orientated e.g. writing letters to school, confidence in visiting the doctor, making telephone calls. In this case we can immediately spot the competence that would relate to an appropriate level for the student.

Others may be far less closely defined, such as improving writing or reading. Then we will need to be diagnostic in our approach at the outset and find out what stage the student is already at and what difficulties may be presenting themselves. It may be that out of this the short term learning goals are orientated – learning the past tense, the passive, or vocabulary for everyday life. However, though the learning itself will be language specific the student will still need to practise it in the context of communication. It is in this practice that an assessment of competence can be made. In this way the accreditation is incidental yet relevant.

The Standards and learning needs

To show how the Standards can be relevant to students needs we will look at some different individuals' learning situations. In each of these cases, with accompanying case studies, the student's long term goals and subsequent assessment of learning needs have identified situations where in the learning programme:

- the acquisition of basic skills predominates

- the development of language predominates

- there is a mixture of need

- the student wants/needs accreditation.

Where the acquisition of basic skills predominates

> **Case Study**
>
> Mrs. H. is Punjabi speaking and has lived in England for 15 years. Her spoken English is competent enough for her to lead a full everyday life and to work in a factory. She is not literate in Punjabi and has never written English. She can read signs and some words and simple sentences though holding the information she reads, in order to fully understand it, is difficult. She had virtually no schooling because of family difficulties and her own illness as a child.
>
> She wants to improve her English as she feels there are opportunities for promotion at work. She would need to do some reading and writing in these jobs.

For this student the gradual acquisition of Foundation Level Wordpower would seem to be advantageous. It would give motivation to the learning and provide her employers with proof of competence in a recognised accreditation and give her the chance to learn basic written communication skills which she has not had the chance to learn and develop in mother tongue. This possibility was discussed with the student and a learning programme was negotiated.

Learning Programme

First 6 months

An initial structured approach to reading and writing which started with the alphabet, moved to simple vocabulary and then simple positive and negative statements, gradually increasing the complexity. This was all done through using audio tapes and drilling exercises whereby the student was building up a mental store of visualised language. Small amounts of learning were given on tape, reinforcing what was written on the worksheet. The student was then asked to write the sentence in response to what was heard. At first the words were picked out of the worksheet in response to what was heard, and copied. Gradually the student could call upon her own mental store of 'visualised' words.

By stages the student was beginning to perform everyday tasks in reading and writing. There were few problems in establishing her understanding of text by verbal questioning as her oral competence was high. However, she needed practice in reading to *understand*; in holding and interpreting the information. As this student had no experience of studying she needed help too in reading and understanding instructions.

Gradually she was taking responsibility for achieving Foundation competences.

She brought in a newspaper article, an advertisement that she wanted to write a reply to, and a need to write an advert for the sale of an electric cooker. For this student certain competences such as the oral ones were easily proved but were nevertheless

Element 4·1

To give condition and price (2 Seperate ideas).

FOR   SALE
A Electric cooker
good condition only a
year old - reason FOR
Saleing I am going away
asking only £150 pounds
or near ofer

Tutors remarks.
Purpose sufficiently clear ✓
Understood by reader ✓
Legible ✓

Student asked to simplify to the point where
she was certain of spelling and to write
more clearly.

Element 4·2

I did read alot but I didn't do much
writing because I have to work alot of
overtime. I am sorry. I couldn't come to
college. I did some painting in the
house. My son RAJINDER been on holiday
for two weeks.
I did some Sewing

Sensible order? Understood ✓ Legible ✓ Corrections ✓

To be submitted with other writing.
Practise of sequencing ideas.

Examples of Ms. H's work nearly 12 months after she first started in the Basic Skills Open
Learning Centre.

relevant to her learning programme as they were done as incidentally as possible. Her oral competence enabled her to easily explain procedures and ask for information from other students and thus the competences were recorded. These situations did not need to be 'set up' but happened quite naturally.

Some hints on using The Standards with the long term improver

The way in which the possibility of accreditation is introduced to the long term improver becomes important.

First the tutor needs to ascertain whether the possibility of accreditation is relevant to the student as an individual. Will its 'currency' be meaningful? Will the student appreciate the on-going preparation of a portfolio? Will the possibility of a certificate at the end motivate the student?

The process of Wordpower accreditation must be acceptable and meaningful to the student. However, there may be little point in getting bogged down in the details early on. There may be all sorts of reasons why 'accreditation' and 'performance' and 'assessment' are not acceptable terms to the student. The tutor has to be sensitive to the students' feelings, involving them as much or as little in the process as is appropriate.

In some cases it may be more productive to allow some evidence accumulation just 'to happen' and share the possibility of accreditation at a later stage.

It will, in any case, be a good idea to record on students' work which competences are evidenced in it. These pieces of work would have been completed anyway so why not give them competence-based meaning? They can then be used as evidence at a later stage or stored in a portfolio that the student can take on to a subsequent learning or employment situation.

There is a danger with the long term improver that the possibility of accreditation becomes the driving force. The whole process then can become one of doing worksheets and ticking boxes. This can be overcome by allowing the student to learn in different ways so that:

- some of the work is done in a group where others are also doing Wordpower

- some is done through short course provision

- some is done in an open learning centre or drop-in workshop.

It will also help if the student is encouraged to do some project work on a topic which in itself will allow several competences at once to be satisfied. Where such access to different modes of study is not available then as many of these opportunities as possible need to be available within the group setting. This means that tutors and managers need to be flexible in their use of time, materials and modes of learning within any particular 'session'. It also means that tutors need to be really familiar with the Standards so that they can always be spotting when evidence of the competence has been shown.

40

Where the development of language predominates

Case Study

Ms. I has lived in England for 10 years. Because she has been busy raising a family during this time she has not had the time and motivation to spend on language learning. However, she has acquired a very competent use of everyday language which, though often inaccurate, carries the desired message. She had full schooling, post-school training in catering, and has competent basic and study skills in mother tongue estimated to be equivalent to Wordpower Level 1/2.

She has come to a stage in life when she wishes to improve her employment prospects, her self-confidence, and her role in society. She is keen to perfect her English and to be discriminating in the use of language for different purposes. It is obvious that she will want to spend much of her time in practising writing for everyday tasks in conveying ideas and opinions and putting forward a case.

Learning programme

A diagnostic approach to assessing her needs indicated that she could improve her general vocabulary, her use of tense, her use of expressions, her pronunciation and intonation and her oral presentation skills. A programme of work was devised which addressed:

- specific language learning

- the use of tapes for certain pronunciation and intonation exercises

- some planned interactive work on giving and receiving instructions with another student.

For this student it was important to try and find the ways in which she was using and applying her English outside the learning situation so that she could be accredited more fully. Some of the tasks that were performed in the learning situation were accredited e.g. a paired situation where she was involved with another student in giving instructions to him on constructing a model. This was recorded on tape for the evidence and 16.1 could be accredited. Fortuitously, she became involved in setting up a Family Takeaway business and the mapping of competence is illustrated.

The missing elements 16.1, 2. 3. and 4 of Stage 2 (Providing, Obtaining and Exchanging Information and Opinions) were made up in planning a group activity, with other students also wanting such practice, around a presentation and discussion on banning smoking in all public places.

41

12 Robins Road
Cheltenham
Gloucestershire
GL16 1HZ

Ms A.L. Robinson
Personnel Officer
Baxter Freight Services
4-5 Westgate Road
Gloucester

Dear Ms Robinson

Ref: Application for the post of Catering Assistant

I'm very interested in the above position which you advertised in the Gloucester News on 7th June. I would like to apply for the post. I am a 47 year-old female. I was born in Singapore but I have been living in England for 10 years.

I have experience in catering in Singapore where I was employed to cook for a family and their employees and I can cook a variety of meals.

At present I am a lunchtime supervisor working at The Priory Infant School (in Cheltenham). I have been there for nearly five years. I wanted to change my job because I have got more time to spare now that my children are older. I look forward to hearing from you.

Yours sincerely

Mrs F. Chang

Student performing at Stage 1 but learning programme designed – to work towards Stage 2. This student passed Pitman's Intermediate (Level 3) two years ago.

A real-life example of a student who helped set up a family business (a Chinese Take-away). The Wordpower Units/Elements she actually met in the process. See this chart.

Dealing with the Gloucester County Council
re: council tax form **U10 E1 S1**
U10 E2 S1
S2 U15 E15.1

health and hygiene **U10 E1 S1**

Dealing with the Insurance Company

• public liability insurance policy
(covering staff, food and equipment)

Contact: telephone   **U10 E1 S1**
face-to-face **U10 E2 S1**

forms/letters **U15 E1 S2**
U15 E2 S2
U15 E3 S2

Employing staff

• advertising **S2 U15 E15.2**
• interviewing   **S1 U10 E10.1**
S1 U10 E10.23

SETTING UP A FAMILY BUSINESS

Dealing with the bank

• applying for a business loan **S1 U9 E9.1**
• filling in forms **S2 U15 E15.1**
• setting up a busines account
S2 U15 E15.1

Publicity

• advertising opening **S2 U15 E3**
• promoting offers **S2 U15 E4**
• writing menu **S2 U15 E2**

Dealing with the Solicitor

• lease for the shop
S2 U10 E10.1
S1 U8 E8.1, 8.2

Dealing with the Suppliers

• (conducted in M.T. – Chinese speaking wholesalers)
• letters to creditors
U4.1
S1 U4.1

An example of accreditation of skills with an expectation of learning and improvement in use of language. Set at Stage 1 with expectation of achieving Stage 2.

43

Where there is a mixture of need

Such students may need to concentrate their efforts generally on a mixture of language acquisition, basic skills acquisition and also on study skills. They may also have limited experience of Britain, its systems and a general knowledge of this.

Case Study

Ms. G has come to England from Portugal to marry. She has had limited education because of childhood illness and though literate in mother tongue has not had much chance to build on basic skills and lacks ability to concentrate on learning. She has already acquired some English in a rather haphazard way, primarily through vocabulary which she indiscriminately puts together in both the written and spoken word. A very structured approach to learning is essential but she needs something to motivate her learning, and to help her to concentrate and persist.

Student asked to write about an accident she had seen yesterday.

This Stage 1 assessment revealed that the student needed to do Foundation Level with an emphasis on tasks which required her to simplify and check accuracy.

Additional work on this would not be productive as she needed to be performing at a Foundation Level on Foundation Level tasks.

Learning Programme

With this student it became important to establish the areas of English usage in her everyday life where she wanted to be as accurate as possible as this student needed to monitor her own use of English if she was to improve. Accuracy in written English was important to her but it was obvious that her competency in spoken communication was also badly affected by the jumbled use of words.

This student needed lots of practice in everyday speaking tasks eg. making appointments, asking for help, and giving personal information, where she was simplifying and restricting her use of language to making it accurate in word order, form and intonation. She also needed clearly defined parameters for her use of English in written tasks. Wordpower provided structure to each of the tasks performed and to the overall plan of basic skills to be learned and practised. It provided the added incentive of accreditation. Thus performance criteria could be shared very positively with this student in encouraging accuracy and self-monitoring.

Where the need for accreditation predominates

Such students come because they desire some form of accreditation to certify their current competence. They may want a job, or to gain entry to a college or training course, where such accreditation is required. Sustaining motivation, and gaining evidence for accreditation as easily and quickly as possible, are important factors.

The student will soon lose interest and motivation if he/she just follows through the competences of wordpower producing evidence by using the worksheets already available in the learning situation. Finding a project which will satisfy the student in terms of interest and motivation, and yet provide much evidence less pointedly, is one way. If the programme also runs short courses in response to arising needs where Wordpower accreditation can be awarded for tasks done on the course, then this provides further and more varied opportunities.

Case Study

Mr. V. is attending a Workplace Basic Skills programme. Wordpower is recognised in the factory where he works because of the high profile it has been given during the Basic Skills at Work programme. Subsequently, there has been an on-going Basic Skills provision paid for by the employer which encourages accreditation. As yet there are no obvious spin-offs in employment incentives given for those completing the certificate, though its recognition by the management means a great deal in self-esteem for employees.

Learning programme

Initial assessments showed that this student should be entering at Stage 1. To aim for Stage 2 at this point would have put too high a demand on him for additional learning and practice. He wished to have verification of current abilities.

In order to address this need for accreditation as easily and quickly as possible it was important to ascertain from the tasks performed in his everyday work which competences were being satisfied and for which evidence could be obtained. In his supervisory role he could easily obtain evidence for Unit 8 (Completing Forms and Preformatted documents) and Units 10 and 11 (Conversing with One Other Person and with More than One Person).

It was decided between tutor and student that he would do a project around golf which he had just started to play. This would include

- a short history of golf

- his and his friends reasons for choosing golf as an activity

- a journey plan to two of the nearest courses

- a list of equipment needed (which he needed to reference)

- his following pictorial instructions for a new stroke and reporting on it.

It was decided that Unit 12 could be covered at a later date either within the project e.g. watching a golfing video, or in the workplace during TQM (Total Quality Management) training.

The student himself was responsible for gathering suitable books and materials for the project.

Summary

In using the Standards with long term improvers there are several points to be borne in mind:

- use them so that they are not dominating the activities of the student by

  - determining what tasks and activities will motivate the student and looking for competences within those

  - making sure that as many elements as possible can be evidenced together in one piece of work/task

  - ascertaining how much evidence can be obtained from outside the learning situation

  - provide for and encourage students to do short courses and projects where accreditation can happen more incidentally.

- make sure that the students' personal language development and progress is also recorded in some way so that such language acquisition is recognised by both tutor and student. This means that:

- an adequate initial assessment of use of language should be made
- language itself in terms of grammar, vocabulary and expressions should be part of the students' learning programme.

- make sure that the student is taking as much responsibility as possible for the accreditation process by:

  - expecting that he/she will produce evidence away from the teaching situation as independently as possible
  - encouraging him/her to bring in relevant examples to be worked on
  - facilitating independent learning and completion by providing self-study opportunities within group sessions and/or in a drop-in session or open learning.
  - making learning resources and certain possibilities for gaining accreditation self-accessible.

THE BASIC SKILLS STANDARDS AND THE TRAINEE

Students in this category will be motivated by the occupational demands and the training course demands which themselves will be vocational. This means that much of the basic skills needs of trainees will be specific in the context in which they are learned and practised.

Unfortunately, funding for accreditation has pushed training managers into providing Wordpower accreditation which either totally dominates the trainees' activities by being the 'driver', or becomes a separate entity in the training when the student goes off elsewhere 'to do Wordpower'. It is particularly difficult for ESOL trainees who will already have as part of their action plan that they work on language. This language work too easily becomes 'Wordpower' and the inevitable churning out of accreditation evidence by rote. They become bored and disillusioned as they see no evidence of a real improvement in their language.

This is such a pity when the arena of training for a vocation must lend itself to accrediting trainees with basic skills that they are proving they are competently using in the performance of the vocational tasks on their courses.

There are several reasons for this failure:

- Wordpower accreditation is being seen as a learning programme rather than an accreditation framework. Thus, it is assumed that trainees will **learn** basic communication skills and the English language by just doing Wordpower at Foundation Level.

- No definite place in the action plan is being given to the trainees' individual learning needs in terms of language **and** basic communication skills.

- Funding forces training managers into taking easy short cuts by laying on something 'in addition' rather than examine how there could be an integration of the accreditation process and the individual learning needs into the training course itself.

Where there are trainees who are speakers of other languages there are certain minimum opportunities that should be available to the training course for it to function effectively (Ref. 'Open for Training' NFER and 'Working with Language' NFER):

1. Where possible a bilingual assessor should be used to ascertain the trainees' needs so that there is a distinction between the language needs, the basic skills needs, and the occupational skills needs.

2. Language specialists should be available to ascertain the language demands of the training course, the language levels required by assessment procedures, and the language demands of the occupation.

3. Language must be taught and integrated into the training according to the advice given by the specialists.

4. There must be additional opportunities for those trainees who have specific difficulties with language (e.g. where pronunciation is interfering with the student's competence) and/or with basic communication skills (e.g. following or giving instructions sequentially, picking out important information). These trainees need more time and practice individually. This has implications for the training in that these trainees' needs must be diagnosed and analysed, and a programme of study synthesised for them. This will inevitably demand expertise, time, and a wide range of appropriate, interesting and accessible learning materials.

There is no 'easy answer' to acquiring language and communication skills. Wordpower cannot and should not be expected to address this. Where Wordpower is used it also needs to be integrated much more into what the training course is providing. This also has implications for staff training which enables the trainers to spot when basic skills competences are being fulfilled on the training course. They must be familiar enough with the framework and the performance criteria to facilitate this. The main thrust of the learning should be related to the vocational demands and the content as related to this. Thus, that should be the starting point. In many cases this will relate to the competences of the vocation.

Example: A Training Course for Industrial Machinists

Occupational Task   •   Use Sewing Machine

Some Competences   •   Thread Machine Correctly

                     •   Change Needle on Machine

                     •   Understand Safety Instructions for Machine

In order to try and analyse where basic skills competences might be fulfilled we need to:

- Look at what and how the underpinning knowledge and understanding will be delivered to the trainee.

  Will it be a demonstration, an instruction sheet, a handout etc.?

  The student will need to assimilate this.

  Are any basic skills competences fulfilled?

- Examine any practice exercises the student will do.

  Will the student do any referencing, reading, oral work for this?

  Are any basic skills competences fulfilled?

- Analyse the assessment task for competence and the evidence of competence.

  Is it an oral task or a written task?

  Are any basic skills competences fulfilled?

Example

For the 'threading correctly' competence we may decide that:

Underpinning knowledge is given by a demonstration. (5.2.).

Practice exercises are given with pictorial instructions in stages (2.4.)
Trainees should label parts of machine
They should describe it to one another (5.1. and 5.3)

The **assessment task** is drawing the position of the thread on a drawing of the machine. Instructions on how to do this task are written (1.2).

At **each** of these stages it is possible to collect evidence of competence for the Wordpower elements. It is not only at the stage of assessment for the occupational task that the trainee is showing that basic communication skills are being used competently, but at **all** stages in the process.

ESOL Introduction to Sewing Course and Wordpower (Gloscat)

Standards	Worksheet title	Assessment	Comment
F3.2/3.1	Fill in Enrolment forms	completed form	
F5.1	Parts of the Body	oral questions from tutor	first try
F5.1/5.2	Starting to make a paper pattern	oral pairwork written record	second try
F1.2	Getting to know your sewing machine	oral task written record (labelling)	
I,6.2	Threading the machine	presentation to group	
2.4	Raising the Bobbin thread	task	
1.2	Threading the sewing machine	task, pictorial evidence	
2.4	Changing machine parts		
2.3	Choosing the right needle	oral or written	select part of the table for assessment
1.1 5.1	Sewing machine safety instructions	reading with oral or written assessment	oral assessment for F5.1
5.2	Measurements test	oral task, written record	pairwork or student/tutor
I,1.2 (F1.2)	Drawing out a paper pattern 1 & 2	task, pattern as evidence	If exercise is oral presentation from tutor, then F1.2
F1.2	Necklines	task, pattern as evidence	
F1.2 I,1.2	Sleeve pattern	task, pattern as evidence	'Bridge' between F & Stage 1 – progression in portfolio
F2.3 F3.1/3.2	Buying Material 1	conversion task simple form filling	Check portfolio for more variety of forms
F5.1/5.2/ 5.3	Buying Material 2	Free role play after scripted practice	script provides vital practice for intonation and meaning though not assessed by WP
F1.1 & F4.1	Buying Material 3	reading play Q & A in writing	could be done orally omitting 4.1
F2.4	Wiring a plug	task, finished plug as evidence	
F2.3	Electrical Appliances & equipment	reading table written evidence	
F2.1	Washing Symbols Exercises	written evidence	could be done orally

SEWING MACHINE 1

Name: ....

Date: ....

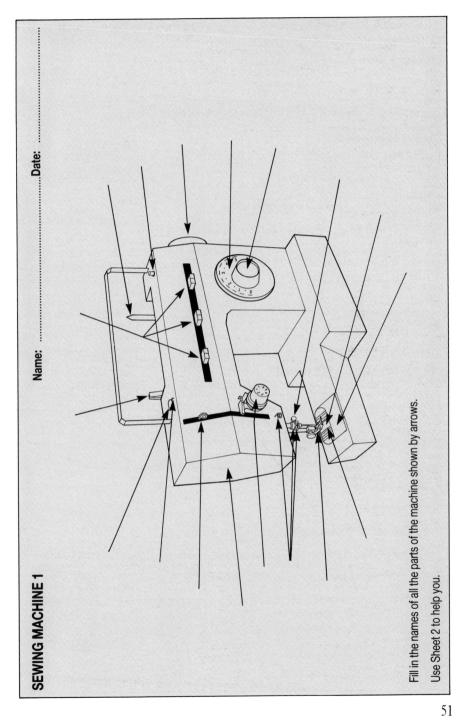

Fill in the names of all the parts of the machine shown by arrows.

Use Sheet 2 to help you.

COURSE TITLE – A Parent/Carers Role in Pre-School Learning

from Ell Jaggi *'Making Training Work'*

An example from the course.

i) Course content.

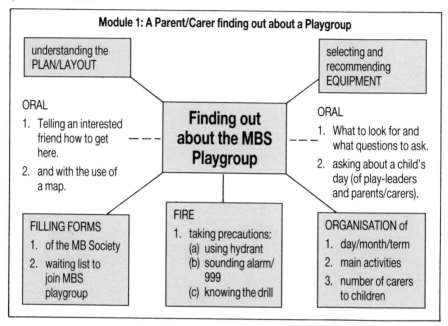

ii) Language which will be covered:

LANGUAGE to be taught and practised.

Key functions

- **Instruction: e.g.** how and when to wean a baby.

- **Description: of slide, e.g.** and swing – orally and in a letter.

- **Description: of process, e.g.** how to make playdough.

- **Narrative: e.g.** stories from the past to tell children.

- **Giving and getting information, advice, assistance and permission: e.g.** about different toys and aids to physical, emotional or creative development; replying to an invitation to a birthday party and asking for a present (a toy) to be sent by mail order.

- **Classifying: e.g.** kinds of toys.

- **Complaining: e.g.** about a milk bill.

iii) Tasks which students will perform in acquiring information for the 'content', practising language, and presenting information.

TASKS and Wordpower Accreditation		
WEEK 1: 3793 Communication Skills (Wordpower) Foundation Level – May 10-13. *(See Module for Week 1)*		
Number of activity and type:		
1. Find the way using a map or plan.	Unit 002	Element 2a & 1a
2. Refer to written instruction to carry out an activity. (using shampoo on babies 0 – 5)	Unit 001	Element 2a
3. Read through the document to establish what is required.	Unit 003	Element 1a
4. Fill in the form (MBS + Playgroup form).	Unit 003	Element 2a & 2b
5. Refer to written instructions to carry out an activity (i) Explain instruction on fire hydrant. (ii) Written fire drill; write, learn and carry out activity.	Unit 001	Element 2b
+		
6. Obtain information from playgroup leader, as to how it's organised, its main activities in the day/month/term; and number of carers to children).	Unit 005	Element 2
7. Provide information to a friend who wants to send her toddler to the playgroup as to whose it is and why it is a good place to send her baby.	Unit 005	Element 1

THE BASIC SKILLS STANDARDS AND THE STUDENT WHO COMES FOR SPECIFIC PURPOSES

In the ESOL situation students will often come for very specific reasons:

- they are now alone at home and wish to be able to answer the telephone competently

- they are wanting to work in the family shop and need to talk with customers at the till

- they have a chance of promotion which will mean that they will do some receptionist duties and want to practise this.

If their learning programme restricts itself firmly to these scenarios there are few competences which could be achieved. However, as tutors we should be looking for every possibility for accreditation if it is relevant and appropriate. Each of these situations could be expanded productively to include writing tasks, e.g. taking messages and reading tasks e.g. reading instructions, responding to letters. The students will still be practising tasks that are relevant to why they have come. They will therefore be motivated. All this must be explained and negotiated with the student, but once again it is a more incidental acquisition of accreditation which could itself be motivating.

THE BASIC SKILLS STANDARDS AND THE LEARNING/STUDY SUPPORT STUDENT

When a tutor is supporting a student on a mainstream college course it is necessary for the tutor

- to establish about the course itself:

  - the level of basic communication skills demanded of the student in understanding and interpreting information given in delivery of the course (lectures, handouts, textbooks, audiovisual material)

  - the level of basic communication skills demanded of the student by the assessment procedures

  - the level of basic communication skills demanded of the student in the presentation of written and spoken material

  - the specific language demands (specific vocabulary, expressions, grammatical structures required, etc)

- to ascertain about the student:

  - level of current performance in basic communication skills

  - level of current use of English.

The tutor is then able to spot the gaps in the student's performance and address these in a learning programme which is related to course demands.

The ALBSU standards and Wordpower can provide the learning/study support situation with a framework in which to ascertain gaps, spot ways of helping students

54

to fill these gaps, and subsequently enable the student to gain a step-by-step accreditation for the work which is done in this support learning.

Case study

Mr. R., a 30 year old Moroccan, has enrolled on a BTEC National Business and Finance course and is advised by course tutors to make contact with study support for help with his assignments.

He is used to studying, is qualified as a surveyor, learned English at school, and has been working in a cafe for two years. He now wants to gain business qualifications in England.

The core skills covered in the assignment which he is currently doing are at GNVQ Level 3. This has been equated to Stage 3 Wordpower in mapping exercises *(See table on page 6).*

The assignment is about marketing vegetables. Some articles with information about potatoes have been provided as source material and the student is asked to choose a variety (make a judgement) to market and then write a 500 word interesting and informative article to support the choice; stating benefits to the purchaser; likely competition; and existing market possibilities. At Level 3 (of GNVQ) the information given for the task (from newspaper and research articles) is 'freely structured' and from a variety of documents. This demands a high level of reading, extracting, and assimilating. The presentation in the form of an article requires that the student him/herself determines the structure calling upon high level productive skills and logical order.

Compare GNVQ Level 2 and 3 for READING

Level 2
GNVQ Element 2.4 Read and respond to written material and images on routine matters (e.g. day to day organisation and administration) –presented in preset *formats,* outline *formats* (memos, letters, report cards, etc)

Level 3
GNVQ Element 3.4 Read and respond to written material and images on a range of matters (e.g. a report on a piece of research) – presented *freely structured* (wide variety of documents – books, formal reports *i.e. so that information extraction is complex).*

Compare GNVQ Level 2 and 3 for WRITING

Level 2
GNVQ Element 2.2 Prepare written material on routine matters in *pre-set (forms)* or outline *formats* (letters, reports).

55

Level 3

GNVQ Element 3.2 Prepare written material on a range of matters including complex and non-routine matters (e.g. report on a piece of research) in a format including *freely structured* documents (where structure is determined by the individual).

<table>
<tr><td colspan="2"></td><td>LEVEL 2</td><td>LEVEL 3</td></tr>
<tr>
<td rowspan="9">READING</td>
<td>READING TEXTUAL MATERIAL</td>
<td>13.1 Choose and use appropriate material from more than one written source.</td>
<td rowspan="2">17.1 Select and evaluate material from a wide variety of written texts.</td>
</tr>
<tr>
<td rowspan="3">READING GRAPHICAL MATERIAL FOR EVERYDAY PURPOSES</td>
<td>13.2 Select material from more than one graphical source (e.g. complex tables, plans).</td>
</tr>
<tr>
<td rowspan="2">13.3 Understand the purpose and meaning in a text and make a judgement from the information.</td>
<td rowspan="2">17.2 Find and interpret information which is presented in graphical and textual form.</td>
</tr>
<tr></tr>
<tr>
<td rowspan="2">USING REFERENCE SYSTEMS</td>
<td>14.1 Use a reference system to find specific information (e.g. find a book in a library or a file in a filing system).</td>
<td>18.1 Use a range of reference systems (e.g. using a library to find a variety of material in order to research a topic).</td>
</tr>
<tr>
<td>14.2 Organise material into a given reference system – alphabetical, numerical or date order and use the system created.</td>
<td>18.2 Select and create a reference system.</td>
</tr>
<tr>
<td rowspan="5" style="writing-mode: vertical">WRITING</td>
<td>COMPLETING FORMS AND PREFORMATTED DOCUMENTS</td>
<td></td>
<td></td>
</tr>
<tr>
<td rowspan="2">COMMUNICATING IN WRITING</td>
<td>15.1 Complete forms requiring detailed information (e.g. accident report form).</td>
<td rowspan="2">19.1 Write in a variety of styles and formats to convey complex information and opinions.</td>
</tr>
<tr>
<td>15.2 Write material in a specialised format (e.g. curriculum vitae, formal letters, leaflets).</td>
</tr>
<tr>
<td>15.3 Write in a variety of styles to convey information and opinions on everyday or familiar issues.</td>
<td rowspan="2">19.2 Write vividly and effectively in appropriate lengths and depths to convey ideas, feelings and experiences.</td>
</tr>
<tr>
<td>15.4 Write effectively to convey ideas, feelings and experiences.</td>
</tr>
</table>

Thus we see that at the Level 3 that a speaker of another language may cope well with the receptive skills of reading at Level 3 but may well be hindered in writing by use of language. This is where the ALBSU standards as used in Wordpower can be helpful to tutors in sorting out the difficulties that exist between the possession of **skills** and the posession of **language**. The skills are broken down into smaller steps than are indicated in GNVQ so that it is easier to find gaps.

Look at the example of Mr. R's work for this (see page 58). It is obvious from this that Level 3 is not being achieved.

By using the ALBSU standards which relate to GNVQ Level 2 and 3 we can see that Mr.R could achieve Stage 3 for the Reading Textual and Graphical Material (Unit 17). His written answer and questioning by the tutor shows that he has selected and extracted information to make a judgement and for a specific purpose.

However, we need to look more closely at his writing. It is also obvious that he could do some immediate work on sentence structure and word order and that he needs to learn to proof read and experiment with simplifying his use of language. But, he also needs help in structuring and conveying information. He needs a lot of practice at Stage 2 Wordpower Unit 15 Communicating in Writing.

By providing him with a format (applicable to GNVQ Level 2) and an expectation of accuracy with simplified structures he should learn the skill of stating facts simply and logically. All his practice material should be at Stage 2 until he has mastered the **skills** at this level. The underpinning knowledge and understanding which is stated with the performance criteria will also help us to plan the learning programme. At the same time his learning programme must address grammar, sentence structure and vocabulary. He could spend time on learning and practising some standard expressions:

e.g. One advantage of.....is....

One reason to choose ..... is that.....

Learning programme

1. A short comprehension with questions which ask only about factual content. Mr. R is asked to write whole sentence answers in a grammatical form that he is certain is correct.

    Any major grammatical difficulties are picked up and addressed.

2. Student asked to look back at assignment and asked to tackle it in this way:

    The product...... was chosen because it ....

    For each of these – availability
                         – yield
                         – profits
                         – uses

The product choosed is Desiree this Product was choosen because mamy reasons they vary from one reason to another - one it could be the avaibility of the product around the year- and total Production of this kind of product as we can in leaflet of Potato statistics bulletin (of Potato Marketing board) in Maicrop is about good record of 7,148 hectares which is not bad propotion if we compare with the rest of the Potato Products.

From Point of view of the total area Planted by registered Products Desiree is just around between 4% n 5% of total Plantings but its probably something to do withe prices of the other products

So the benefits that the selected variety will bring the purchaser is nose of profits with more people asking for this product because of its competitive prices the product is harvested in September -May which good time or by other uneaning maincrop group which long time to produce them which influence on the price as well & Desiree is good for all cooking purposes which is an advantage for the product The selected variety has got realistic competitors it could be price &long avaibility of this Product & the qualities of divession of cooking - aims.

Write one sentence using the structure above.

Check then correct.

Under each of these then write a sentence:

This means that...........

Then try writing a paragraph:

The advantages to the purchaser

Use this structure:
This variety is a good one to buy because
it will ....
it can....

Summary

So how have Wordpower and the ALBSU standards helped in learning support with this student?

1. They have helped us to give a starting point to his learning – we have 'placed' him at level 3 for reading and 2 for writing. From this we can measure his progress. We have made an 'initial' assessment.

2. They have helped us to identify the gaps in his skills. We can also use the underpinning knowledge and understanding to pinpoint further what he can valuably spend time on.

3. They have helped us to identify the level of learning material he should be working with so that he can build on this. Continually presenting him with material above his current skills level (in this case at Stage 3 which is equivalent to his course) will stunt progression.

4. They have given us the framework in which to chart his progress. We can make statements about this learning progress, in terms of competence, using the standards.

5. The student has the chance of being accredited for Basic Skills as a recognition of the effort which has been put in for study support.

The Basic Skills Standards and the beginner

This category refers to students who are beginners in learning the English language. They may or may not have basic communication skills in mother tongue. If they are not literate in mother tongue then they will not have had a chance to develop skills in the written word. However, it is quite possible that a beginner may have very advanced communication skills in mother tongue. For such students in both categories the over-riding motivator is to acquire enough English for them to cope and survive.

The first step with such students is to enable them to acquire a good foundation in English which addresses everyday tasks and a grammatical basis from which they can develop the language. The Standards are relevant to the situations and tasks that they will perform in practising English.

However, it may require some time to be spent on the underpinning language for some time before accreditation can be attempted.

For instance a beginner needs for both spoken and written language:

- basic vocabulary

- understanding and use of verb 'do' in questions and negatives

- appreciation of role played by word order

- an appreciation of tense.

5 | Implications for programmes

Practitioners are using Wordpower and the ALBSU standards within programmes:

- **as accreditation**

    - sometimes as an additional competence-based possibility where other exam-based qualifications are already available such as Pitman ESOL, the Cambridge series KET, PET, First Certificate and Proficiency.

    Offering Wordpower additionally allows students who have never previously developed basic skills to build up to accreditation gradually and enables all ESOL students to compete on an equal footing with mother tongue English speaking students.

    - sometimes to provide accreditation alongside training or a mainstream vocational course. Here the students benefit from basic skills accreditation as much of the student effort is going into improving basic skills and it is thus recognised.

    - sometimes as accreditation more incidentally alongside a basic skills short course or linked skills course. These courses have specific learning outcomes and by the very nature of the course the student can be accredited for the basic skills they have developed and used competently as part of the course.

- **as a framework** for placing students' initial competence and charting their learning progress. As funding, and therefore management, become more learning-outcome orientated having such a framework becomes vital. For the ESOL student using such a framework alone is insufficient as it does not chart language development in language terms. However, it does provide a framework which can be applied across the basic skills provision as a whole.

Accreditation and the programme

If accreditation is to be meaningful in programmes it should have a significant profile but still not dominate the basic skills teaching and organisation which it may do if 'Wordpower' groups, courses and resources become central. It should not drive the delivery but permeate the provision in a way that it can open up accreditation

61

possibilities to students and trainees at appropriate times. This has implications for ESOL programmes in publicising it and implementing it.

1. giving Wordpower status and a good image, as an accreditation possibility, to encourage students.

2. making sure that all tutors working within the provision are familiar enough with the Standards to spot where students individually can be accredited.

3. providing ample opportunities for students to gain accreditation by a variety of modes and not just in a 'Wordpower group' so that meaningful learning and progression is made by the students.

4. using tutor time effectively in
   - organising the provision
   - group management
   - record keeping
   - giving Wordpower-specific support

5. facilitating progression routes

6. providing a wide range of learning materials and Wordpower-specific materials.

1. Giving Wordpower a good image

Where the ESOL service does not work closely alongside ABE there may be no natural publicity for Wordpower. The service may be more closely allied with the EFL (English as a Foreign Language) provision for overseas students, in which case Cambridge First Certificate and Proficiency may have a higher profile. Wordpower should be publicised alongside all other accreditation with an explanation of its competence-based structure and how this relates to current thinking in NVQ, GNVQ and the National Curriculum.

In some programmes, where there are large numbers of potential students all speaking one mother tongue, translation of an explanation of Wordpower has proved to be very successful. An individual's personal experience of doing Wordpower and written in mother tongue is also helpful. An indication in this of the commitment needed by the student to achieve accreditation and the responsibility demanded of the student in collecting evidence will do much to encourage realistic expectations.

This image and profile of Wordpower should then be carried throughout the institution so that it has meaning for mainstream courses, vocational training and support. Information on the way in which it relates to GNVQ and other accreditation should be widely available.

WORDPOWER
Accreditation of your Language Skills

What is Wordpower?

WORDPOWER is an English Language skills programme. At each stage of the *WORDPOWER* programme you will learn the communication skills you need for studying, working and for daily life in Britain. *WORDPOWER* can help you to make the most of your English Language classes at the H.C.C.

How does Wordpower work?

As you progress through the course, you will receive credits for the work you complete. If you choose to be assessed for the certificate, an assessor from City and Guilds will come to look at your course work when you are ready. Even if you don't finish the course, the credits you **have** gained can be taken with you, or transferred to another college.

How long does Wordpower take?

There is no set amount of time for you to complete the certificate. You can work at your own pace, and enter for the certificate when you and your tutor feel you are ready. However, we aim for you to complete your course work for the certificate within one academic year. (3 terms between September and July).

Why Wordpower?

WORDPOWER is designed and accredited by **City and Guilds**, a nationally recognised examining body. **City and Guilds** certificates are recognised and respected by colleges and employers throughout the UK. A *WORDPOWER* Certificate will indicate to employers and institutions that you have the English Language skills necessary for the training, course, or job you want to enter.

(Hackney Community College)

2. Familiarity of tutors with the ALBSU Standards framework and Wordpower accreditation

If the Standards framework is to permeate and not dominate then tutors and organisers have to become familiar enough with it that they can implement it to accredit students at relevant and appropriate points in the learning and spot when competences are covered. It is obvious that many practitioners have dismissed Wordpower for ESOL students without giving it a fair try. It is dismissed on the grounds of what it does **not** cover rather than what it does cover. In order to understand and use it, tutors need to familiarise themselves with the performance criteria and the framework as a whole,

63

and how the skills interconnect. The most challenging, and yet productive way, of gaining this familiarity is to work with a project, a short course, or a student's folder of work and analyse the tasks performed in terms of the Wordpower criteria.

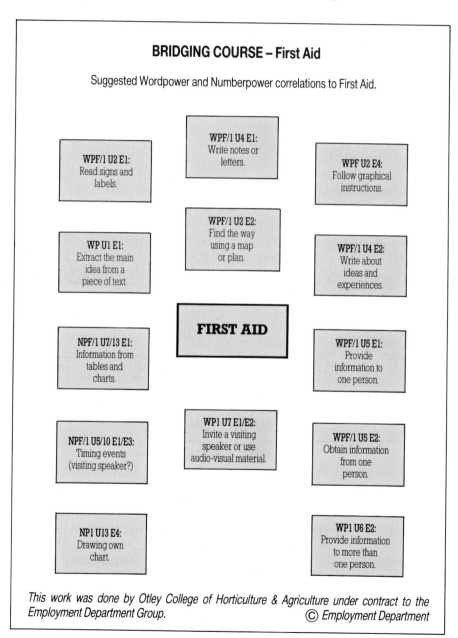

BRIDGING COURSE – First Aid

Suggested Wordpower and Numberpower correlations to First Aid.

WPF/1 U4 E1:
Write notes or letters.

WPF/1 U2 E1:
Read signs and labels.

WPF U2 E4:
Follow graphical instructions.

WPF/1 U2 E2:
Find the way using a map or plan.

WP U1 E1:
Extract the main idea from a piece of text.

WPF/1 U4 E2:
Write about ideas and experiences.

FIRST AID

NPF/1 U7/13 E1:
Information from tables and charts.

WPF/1 U5 E1:
Provide information to one person.

WP1 U7 E1/E2:
Invite a visiting speaker or use audio-visual material.

NPF/1 U5/10 E1/E3:
Timing events (visiting speaker?)

WPF/1 U5 E2:
Obtain information from one person.

NP1 U13 E4:
Drawing own chart.

WP1 U6 E2:
Provide information to more than one person.

This work was done by Otley College of Horticulture & Agriculture under contract to the Employment Department Group. © *Employment Department*

64

Where tutors are familiar with the framework and the performance criteria in general it becomes relatively easy to spot

- when students are incidentally proving a competence in their general learning programme
- when a short course's learning tasks are accreditable
- where competences are fulfilled in a student's project work
- where a course or teaching programme could be expanded or adapted so that accreditation is possible.

Tasks performed by student

- **In gaining underpinning knowledge and understanding**

Task	Basic Skills Competence	Element	Evidence
Look at Picture + Identify dangers from burns	Read signs in pictures	(2·1)	Spoken evidence of identification
Read about burns	Read to extract main point	(1·1)	Fill in questionnaire (3·1) (3·2)

- **In practising skills**

Task	Basic Skills Competence	Element	Evidence
Dealing with a burn — acting it out	Follow pictorial illustrations	(2·4)	Demonstration

- **In assessing the learning**

Task	Basic Skills Competence	Element	Evidence
Role play a scalding accident	Providing and obtaining information	(5·1) (5·2)	Demonstration

Thus, the way to make an analysis of which basic skills competences with Wordpower are fulfilled is first to list the tasks performed then to relate this to competences.

3. Providing different learning opportunities which allow students to accumulate accreditation in a variety of ways

Where we are stuck in our programmes with two hour slots it is easy for us to make over one of these to Wordpower. Then the 'Wordpower group' is born and for ESOL in particular this can then lead to students all doing one element at the same time with a new one being tackled each week. In offering a varied programme with short courses, drop-in tutor supported learning, self-supported sessions, project work, and task orientated study we open up the possibilities for different modes of learning and the accumulation of accreditation. The 'Wordpower group' can then exist as a part of the system in which it is seen as a base where students gain support from a tutor and one another for the other and varied ways in which they are learning and accumulating competences.

Short courses

As there is increasingly more emphasis on learning outcomes it makes sense for provisions to offer short courses in response to identified common needs or interests. In a traditional two-hour a week ESOL group it is possible to have good negotiated learning goals for a limited period of time but then gradually the individual needs and range of abilities in the students take over to such an extent that the group activities lose focus. Hence, the importance of short courses with definite learning aims and outcomes. Such courses will probably cover up to 10 hours of learning.

These courses will have definite content as related to the aims and objectives but as they are essentially about communication skills much of the practice and assessment of learning will be in performing everyday tasks. Thus they lend themselves to enabling the incidental accreditation of competence in performing these tasks. The accreditation framework needs to be superimposed on to the course once its structure and content have been decided.

Examples of short courses

1. *Tenses for intermediate students (4 x 2hrs)*

Session 1

Content – Present tense

Tasks –

1. Use the grammar reference book to find out rules on use of present continuous tense (6.3)

2. Read and act on instructions for task given to you to rearrange the room for a teaching session (6.2)

3. Read an accident report and fill in a form about it (6.1, 8.1, 8.2).

Session 2

Content – Future tense

Tasks –

1. Read holiday plan – write about what you will choose to do (9.1).

Session 3

Content – Past tense

Tasks –

1. Write about your school day experiences and how you felt about them (9.2)

2. Use the tables of day time temperatures. There is also additional information on how much rain there was on April 4, July 20, October 5 and January 8. Use the information to describe the weather on these days. (7.3, 9.1)

and so on . . .

It is important with all short courses that the needs and interests are identified first in the client group and a plan for the course negotiated around this.

Open learning

Some sort of open learning possibility should be available to all students so that they can do additional work on a particular difficulty that they may have, so that they can begin to learn independently, and so that they can access resources with some tutor support as and when they need it for a particular purpose. Programmes need to plan and use their resources to make this possible and to see it as important and integrated part of the whole provision.

For accreditation and Wordpower it also offers:

- an alternative route where the student or trainee him/her self takes much more responsibility for the process and has a supportive atmosphere in which to do this.

- the additional possibility for students or trainees who need to make up a few missing elements for certification.

Other learning opportunities provide interesting opportunities for learning and the possibility of accreditation.

Open Learning Possibility for Safety and First Aid in the Home

This is part of a whole series of interrelated tasks which are for students who have an interest in home safety) *(Gloscat)*.

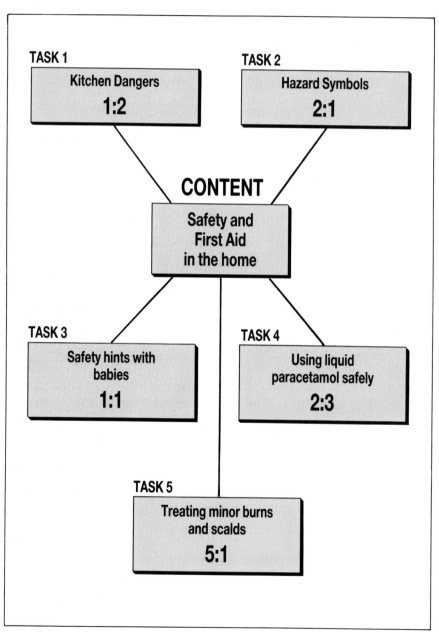

TASK 1
Kitchen Dangers
1:2

TASK 2
Hazard Symbols
2:1

CONTENT
Safety and
First Aid
in the home

TASK 3
Safety hints with
babies
1:1

TASK 4
Using liquid
paracetamol safely
2:3

TASK 5
Treating minor burns
and scalds
5:1

Task 1: Written instructions given to students – Unit 1 Element 2

(a) Look at picture

(b) Find 'dangers'

(c) Circle them with a drawn

(d) Count up the numbers of s

Task 2: Hazard Symbols – Unit 2:1

Task (explained verbally on audio tape) to look at signs and put the relevant number next to the instructions below:

Hazard Symbols

- Poisons to eat or drink – *5 + 6*
- Will easily catch fire – *3 + 4*
- Can explode – *1*
- Is generally harmful or irritant – *7 + 8*

Task 3: Read – Questions asked verbally – UNIT 1:1

SAFETY HINTS WITH BABIES

Safe daily routine

- always put things back in a safe place (e.g. talcum powder)
- don't overfeed the baby

- take baby's bib off after feeding
- use a cat net on the pram

Bath time

- test the water
- never leave baby in a bath alone.

At the toddler stage children need careful supervision, particularly at meal times, going up and down stairs, and where there are dogs and other pets. Beware of silence!

Although children need careful supervision they also need to learn to deal with their home environment. We must also encourage them to learn to keep themselves safe.

Task 4: Dosages of Liquid Paracetamol

Age	Dose
up to 3 months	½ teaspoonful
3 – 12 months	1 teaspoonful
1 – 6 years	1 – 2 teaspoonfuls
over 6 years	up up 3 tsp.

(on audio tape)

- Write down the dose for a baby under 3 months of age.

- What is the dose for a 9 month old baby? Write it down.

- What is the dose for a 7 year old child? Write it down.

- How much would you give a year old child? Write it down.

Task 5: Treating minor burns and scalds – Unit 5 Element 1

Text recorded on audio tape (student also given text). Afterwards student to use pictures to explain to someone else how burns should be treated. Could be recorded on audio tape for tutor to listen through later. Student could explain it to a fellow student who has a checklist of what information should be given.

General Treatment for minor burns and scalds

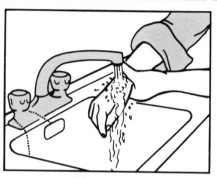

Treatment of burns and scalds depends on the severity of the injury.

1. Place the injured part under slowly running cold water or immerse it in cold water for *at least* 10 minutes.

If no water is available, use any cold, harmless liquid, such as milk or beer instead.

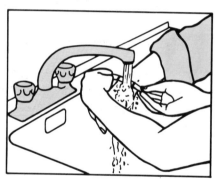

2. Gently remove any rings, watches, belts, shoes or other constricting clothing from the injured area *before* it starts to swell.

3. Dress the area with clean, non-fluffy material.

DO NOT break blisters, remove any loose skin.

DO NOT apply lotions, ointments or fat to the injury.

DO NOT use 'sticky' plasters.

4. If in doubt about the severity of the injury, seek medical aid.

(from St. Johns Ambulance Handbook)

These can be developed independently of the mode of delivery and offer opportunities for groups within groups. Where a two-hour group has become stuck in its development tutors can start by offering the possibility of half the time being 'usual' and half the time different periodically. This opens up the opportunity for the expectation of more independent learning which will be for a significant part of the two-hour slot.

The project

The student would work individually and as independently as possible on a theme which is of particular interest. It is important to structure this at the outset with stages so that the student understands what is expected from him/her. For Wordpower accreditation the tutor needs to have in mind the way in which reading, writing, and oral competences might play a part in the project.

Thus for this:

- the subject area is the starting point

- the tutor ascertains the particular areas of interest for the student

- the tutor thinks about reading writing and oral work that could be involved in the subject area

- these are presented to the student as possibilities and negotiation takes place.

There is a danger with a project that it becomes all written work. This is not only far too restricting from the accreditation point of view but also provides the tutor with far too much student work to read through. Students must be encouraged to produce all sorts of evidence photos, audio tapes, tables, notes etc.

Example

Student's interest = Gardening

Tutor's prompt for Stage 1 to negotiate with student

What changes has the student made recently or will be making in the garden that may have required **reference** work? (**6.3**).

Are there any particular problems facing him/her as a gardener at present

- weeds or insect pests?

- back/health problems?

- tools?

which the student may need to **read** about? (**6.1**).

73

- Will this need treatment and the reading of instructions? (**6.2** and **7.1** and **7.3**).

- How will he/she plan seed sowing/planting this year. Make a chart (**8.1** and **8.2**).

- What gardening programmes does the student see or listen to? (for **12.1** and **2**).

and so on . . .

Reading competences

Negotiate tasks

1. Read about strimmers – cost, safety, weight for two different ones. Student to find information in garden centre – leaflets (6.1,6.3).

2. Find out about mildew and its treatment. Follow treatment procedure. Student to bring all evidence (6.3,6.2,7.1).

and so on . . .

The success of such projects relies on the student's motivation, the reality of the tasks and his/her ability to do much of the work independently and away from the teaching situation. These expectations must be stated and understood from the outset.

The tutor also needs to think through the project in terms of accreditation possibilities. The more familiar the tutor is with the Standards the easier and less time-consuming this becomes. The more independent all students are in the learning situation the more thinking time is available to the tutor.

Once as many competences as possible are fulfilled by the project work the remaining ones needed for accreditation can either be incorporated into the project in some way.

In this example the oral competences could be performed in the basic skills group but using project-based ideas, e.g.:

i) Asking someone about his/her experiences of growing roses 10.1: (Providing information),

ii) Explaining the use of a Strimmer safely 10.3.10.4: Hold a conversation/Support and reassure someone.

Tasks

Within a group setting for two or three sessions running a series of interesting tasks could be presented to the students on which they could collaborate but which would give evidence of competence. If a range of tasks is given requiring a minimum of tutor input and equipment the tutor is then relieved to do other work.

Some of these tasks could be performed away from the teaching situation. The tutor will need to use his/her knowledge of the students abilities to pair them productively.

Audio-taping instructions for the task as well as giving them in a written form will aid understanding.

Examples

Task 1

Use the reference books available (tutor has selected these – dictionary, functional English books, shopping topic book) to work out what you would say to Asda customer services when you return some eggs which taste bad. (6.3) You are angry because this also happened two weeks ago. Help one another to choose the best words, and practise the intonation. Write down the conversation. (10.1,10.3) Fill in complaint form (8.1 and 8.2).

Task 2

(Pictorial instructions could be given for this (2.4.)).

You have some beetroot. You also have some bicarbonate of soda and vinegar. Add each of these to the beetroot. Describe what happens. Use dictionaries if you wish. Then write it down. (2.2, 4.1, 5.1).

Task 3

Look at the two pictures. Decide which one of you will describe picture 1 and who will describe Picture 2. Use dictionaries to help you. Practise first what you will say and then record your description on audio tape. Listen to the recording. What do you want to change about what you said? Record yourselves again. (Element 10.1) Write about the picture you like most describing it and giving reasons for your choice. (Element 9.2).

The purpose of such sessions is to encourage the students to work independently of the tutor and to work collaboratively. The tasks need to be interesting and fun so that they are enjoyed. The reward for the student becomes the completed task and the possibility of accreditation. Students have to rely on reference books and on one another for the language they require rather than on any tutor input. They need to understand that the successful completion of the task is what matters. They do not need to be worried in this instance that their language is not being corrected at every step by the tutor.

These tasks can be self-standing and can therefore be available in an open learning centre so that additional possibilities for completing competences for accreditation are offered.

Self-help groups

Students can be encouraged to meet together and support one another over assembling evidence or finding appropriate materials with as little tutor input as possible. This is most easily facilitated where an open learning opportunity is available. The students will need guidance on what to do step by step for a session but this could be written down or given to them on audio tape.

4. Using tutor time effectively

There are implications for programmes in

- using the total tutor time input more imaginatively

- using tutor-student contact time more productively.

Demands made on the provision to be responsive to need and to encourage imaginative delivery with short courses and drop-in open learning require that the total tutor input time is more flexible than is allowed by a huge dependency on two-hour slots. The very nature of the Wordpower accreditation scheme relies on such flexibility being available to the students/trainees.

However, there will always be programmes and geographical restrictions which will still mean that there is much two-hour provision. Here the tutor needs to be encouraged to be innovative in the use of time within the group so that as many as possible of the advantages of a flexible provision are brought to the student in the two hour slot.

Tutors need help and training for group sessions to:

- prepare them for changes which will encourage students to take more responsibility for their own learning and accreditation

- enable them to manage the student contact time in a way which frees them up for vital administrative work. The requirements now for record keeping with or without Wordpower are such that this is essential.

Record keeping

There must be a recognition by management, practitioners and students of the crucial part record keeping plays in the accreditation process. The time must be found for this and programmes need to sort out and plan for such essential tasks and not just hope that they will 'happen' somehow. For Wordpower thought needs to be given to how well the record keeping can be simplified, how much should be expected of student or tutor, and how much training tutors need to help them to do it. Guidelines to students and tutors will clarify expectations.

Wordpower-specific support

There is some point to in providing specific support to students at the end of their portfolio-building which will give them specific guidance on how to complete it and present it. Some provisions have found it advantageous to plan in some drop-in

		UNIT

Name   Date   Element

FOUNDATION

Pre-task Activity

Task

Performance Criteria

Task One

Comments

sessions with specific Wordpower support at appropriate intervals during the year and to advertise these to all students.

5. Facilitating progression routes

If a student is accredited with competence in basic skills at a particular level it should make it more possible for him/her to progress on to a mainstream course which demands that level of skills at entry. This implies that the institution as a whole is familiar with the ALBSU Standards framework and Wordpower accreditation and that the courses themselves know what level of basic skills are demanded. GNVQ core skills to some extent will provide this sort of help but the skills are not clearly enough separated for it to be of great value in this respect.

Where basic skills delivery in institutions is by full-time or substantially part time courses they can be analysed by topic area for basic skills competences which then will have universal applicability to subsequent courses and be independent of the subject matter (content). The accompanying examples are from Hackney College *(pages 75-78)*.

6. Providing a wide range of learning materials and Wordpower specific materials

The learning resources must:

- provide learning and reference over a wide range

  - language specific subjects (grammar,vocabulary, pronunciation, intonation)

  - general and specific knowledge and information

  - the skills – How to be effective in reading, writing, listening, and speaking.

- be 'known' by the tutors who will be planning learning programmes with the students. It is a good idea to facilitate this in some way by an indexing system.

- be as self-accessible as possible to the students – this means choosing an appropriate range and level for the client group, relevant topics and subjects, and organising them in away which can easily be followed and accessed.

- take account of the different ways in which students might learn

  - task (doing) exercises

  - audio tapes with worksheets (so that that they can listen as well as read)

  - graphical input and explanations instead of text

  - using IT.

This will in turn provide the resources with a framework for relating them to Wordpower and prevented them from becoming literacy-based.

HACKNEY COMMUNITY COLLEGE – ESOL PROGRAMME AREA

WORDPOWER SYLLABUS GUIDELINES – 1993/94

Topic Area: _____   Level: _____

Unit	Element	Task	Scheme Pamphlet Description

HACKNEY COMMUNITY COLLEGE – ESOL PROGRAMME AREA – WORDPOWER SYLLABUS GUIDELINES – 1993/94

Topic Area: **HEALTH**   Level: **FOUNDATION**

Unit	Element	Task	Scheme Pamphlet Description
001	1	Reading a letter from a clinic or hospital / Reading a poster about alcohol or drug abuse	READING TEXTUAL MATERIAL – Extract the main idea from a piece of text.
001	2	Dosages and instructions on medicine bottles	READING TEXTUAL MATERIAL – Refer to written instruction to carry out an activity.
002	1	Medicine labels	READING GRAPHICAL MATERIALS FOR EVERYDAY PURPOSES – Read signs and labels.
002	2	Looking at plan of hospital/clinic	READING GRAPHICAL MATERIAL FOR EVERYDAY PURPOSES – Find the way of using a map or plan.
002	3	Cholesterol chart – Height/weight chart / Baby's growth chart	READING GRAPHICAL MATERIAL FOR EVERYDAY PURPOSES – Extract information from tables.
002	4	First Aid instructions (What to do for burns, etc)	READING GRAPHICAL MATERIAL FOR EVERYDAY PURPOSES – Follow pictorial instructions to carry out an activity.
003	1	Letter telling you what to bring to hospital. Registering with a GP. Reading back of a prescription. Form for giving blood (who can't give blood, etc)	COMPLETING FORMS AND PREFORMATTED DOCUMENTS – Read through the documents to establish what is required.
003	2	As above	As above, plus fill in appropriate forms.
004	1	Writing sick-note to child's school 'Get Well Soon' card.	COMMUNICATION IN WRITING – Write letters, notes and other messages.
003	2	Writing about your own or someone else's illness or accident	COMMUNICATING IN WRITING – Write about ideas and experiences.
005	1, 2, 3	Making an appointment with doctor/dentist. Talking to doctor and getting prescription	CONVERSING WITH ONE OTHER PERSON – Provide info. to one person. Obtain info. Obtain info. from one person. Hold a conversation with one person.

An example of how a college have adapted existing topics (e.g. Health) to accredit them with Wordpower.

HACKNEY COMMUNITY COLLEGE – ESOL PROGRAMME AREA – WORDPOWER SYLLABUS GUIDELINES – 1993/94

Topic Area: **JOBS AND WORK**

Level: **STAGE 1**

Unit	Element	Task	Scheme Pamphlet Description
006	1	To get main points from job adverts in newspaper / Job cards in Job Centre	READING TEXTUAL MATERIAL – Extract information or meaning from a variety of written sources.
006	2	Sending off for an application form / Loading a computer program from disk	READING TEXTUAL MATERIAL – Refer to written instructions to carry out an activity.
006	3	Scan reading for specific qualifications/skills of specific job descriptions / Choosing appropriate vocabulary for CV / Using Yellow Pages	READING TEXTUAL MATERIAL – Consult a reference source to obtain a specific item of information.
007	1	Instructions on how to use a photocopier / Safety notices and signs	READING GRAPHICAL MATERIAL FOR EVERYDAY PURPOSES – Read and act on signs and labels.
007	2	Planning a journey to a job interview	READING GRAPHICAL MATERIAL FOR EVERYDAY PURPOSES – Plan a journey using maps.
007	3	Using a bus/train timetable	READING GRAPHICAL MATERIAL FOR EVERYDAY PURPOSES – Extract information from tables.
008	1	Read a job advertisement/application form	COMPLETING FORMS AND PREFORMATTED DOCUMENTS – Read through the documents to establish what is required.
008	2	Fill in application form	COMPLETING FORMS AND PREFORMATTED DOCUMENTS – Fill in the form.
009	1	Writing a CV/Covering letter / Telephone message for a colleague at work	COMMUNICATING IN WRITING – Write letters, reports, notes and other messages.
009	2	A description of a day at work / Supporting statement	COMMUNICATING IN WRITING – Convey ideas, feelings and experiences in written form.
010	1	Giving information at a job interview	CONVERSING WITH ONE OTHER PERSON – Provide information to one person.

82

HACKNEY COMMUNITY COLLEGE – ESOL PROGRAMME AREA – WORDPOWER SYLLABUS GUIDELINES – 1993/94

Unit	Element	Task	Scheme Pamphlet Description
010	2	Asking questions at job interview Reporting back on job interview Finding out the cost of a classified advertisement	CONVERSING WITH ONE OTHER PERSON – Obtain information from one person.
010	3	Social conversation with colleague at work	CONVERSING WITH ONE OTHER PERSON – Hold a conversation with one person.
010	4	Conversation during first day at work	CONVERSING WITH ONE OTHER PERSON – Support and reassure someone who is in an unfamiliar situation.
011	1	Office Party	CONVERSING WITH MORE THAN ONE PERSON – Perform introductions and farewell.
011	2	Role play – Boss speaking to staff/union representative Showing people around Talking about a particular interest	CONVERSING WITH MORE THAN ONE PERSON – Provide information to more than one person.
012	1	Health and Safety talk	EXTRACTING INFORMATION FROM AUDIO-VISUAL MATERIAL AND LECTURES – Obtain information from a live talk or lecture.
012	2	Programme on safety at work	EXTRACTING INFORMATION FROM AUDIO-VISUAL MATERIAL AND LECTURES – Obtain information from a radio or TV broadest or tape recording.

Using the ALBSU standards for 'placing' students and charting progress

The danger is using the ALBSU standards in this way is that students could feel branded with a level of performance. It is better that the standards are used positively to make competence statements about their current performance. It would be better to state that the student/trainee can 'Convey ideas, feelings and experiences in written form (9.2)' rather than state that 'He/she is at Stage 1 with communication in writing'. Wordpower in this instance is a tool for the tutor, who should be really familiar with the competences at different levels. Thus the tutor will 'place' the student on the framework to enable him/her to analyse and diagnose need, but will translate that position to the student in terms of competence. Subsequently, the tutor will recognise progress in terms of movement in position on the framework but this will be expressed to the student as change in competence statements. The student must be able to recognise progress in the statement itself.

Implications for programmes in using the framework in this way are:

- Recognition of time needed for familiarisation by tutors.

- The competences should also be recognised by mainstream tutors and training managers.

- The ALBSU Standards framework should underpin the provision as a whole.

Staff Development

There are implications for staff development in

- understanding the competence standards so that they can be easily applied

- familiarisation of tutors with learning resources

- tutor's flexible use of time in groups

- record keeping.

The key to making Wordpower work in programmes is the training of all tutors addressing these issues. To an extent they are interdependent. Some programmes where Wordpower is very widely used (e.g. Hackney) build in training time for all tutors. This allows them all to keep abreast of developments and helps them to share ideas. Building in such time is not only possible but desirable for good practice and demands a more imaginative use of tutor time input than occurs in most programmes.

However, such a blanket approach to training can only be effective where there are large numbers of staff and students.

Training is only effective if it comes at the right time. In order to achieve this in smaller programmes it should be made possible for tutors to gain access to the training at an appropriate level and at a time which is relevant to their current working situation. Many of us have undergone Wordpower training at a time when it was not appropriate to our working situation and it was not only wasted but may have discouraged us. There is a place for a self-access learning pack for tutors which would allow the tuors to access training when they are ready and need it.

This does not deny the need for all practitioners who are involved in a Wordpower programme to meet and exchange ideas and work collaboratively on resources and procedures on a regular basis. Time, with the expected outcomes from this 'time', must be built in and honoured if quality and efficacy are to be maintained.

**Bury College
Learning Resources
Woodbury Centre**

The Turn to Biographical Methods in Social Science

Biographical approaches have become increasingly attractive to social scientists as they attempt to account both for individual actions and for social and cultural changes. This book combines an exploration of the origins and development of this methodological 'turn', with examples and analysis from Britain, France and Germany of the different ways that biographical methods have been successfully used and elaborated. Through many illustrative examples of socio-biography in process, the authors show how formal textual analysis, whilst uncovering hidden emotional defences in individual experiencing, can also shed light on wider historical processes of societal transformation. Topics discussed include:

- linking the personal and the social
- generational change and social upheaval
- political influences on memory and identity
- biographical work in reflexive societies
- individual and researcher narratives
- biography and empowerment in professional practice
- typologising, theorising and generalising in case study research.

The Turn to Biographical Methods in Social Science will promote debate and provide models for students and researchers to deepen their understanding and widen their practice of socio-biographical research.

Prue Chamberlayne is Director of the Centre for Biography in Social Policy at the University of East London; **Joanna Bornat** is Senior Lecturer in the Department of Health and Social Welfare at the Open University; **Tom Wengraf** is Senior Lecturer in Sociology and Social Research Methods at Middlesex University.

Social Research Today
edited by Martin Bulmer

The *Social Research Today* series provides concise and contemporary introductions to significant methodological topics in the social sciences. Covering both quantitative and qualitative methods, this new series features readable and accessible books from some of the leading names in the field and is aimed at students and professional researchers alike. This series also brings together for the first time the best titles from the old *Social Research Today* and *Contemporary Social Research* series edited by Martin Bulmer for UCL Press and Routledge. Other series titles include:

Principles of Research Design in the Social Sciences *by Frank Bechhofer and Lindsay Paterson*

Social Impact Assessment *by Henk Becker*

Quantity and Quality in Social Research *by Alan Bryman*

Research Methods and Organisational Studies *by Alan Bryman*

Field Research: A Sourcebook and Field Manual *by Robert G. Burgess*

In the Field: An Introduction to Field Research *by Robert G. Burgess*

Research Design second edition *by Catherine Hakim*

Measuring Health and Medical Outcomes *by Crispin Jenkinson*

Methods of Criminological Research *edited by Victor Jupp*

Information Technology for the Social Scientist *edited by Raymond M. Lee*

An Introduction to the Philosophy of Social Research *by Tim May and Malcolm Williams*

Surveys in Social Research fourth edition *by David de Vaus*

Researching the Powerful in Education *edited by Geoffrey Walford*

Martin Bulmer *is Professor of Sociology and Co-director of the Institute of Social Research at the University of Surrey. He is also Academic Director of the Question Bank in the ESRC Centre for Applied Social Surveys, London.*